ADVANCE PRAISE FOR

BEGINNING WITHIN

Marking a New Journey Toward Equity
in Trauma-Informed Education Practices

"*Beginning Within: Marking a New Journey Toward Equity in Trauma-Informed Education Practices* was a true joy to read. Having recently launched a department focused on student support and behavioral concerns, it validated what I've experienced working with college students and colleagues. It is so important that students feel a sense of belonging and connectedness to enhance their academic success. This book offers thoughtful reflections on just how important this is, how implementing small changes can make a big difference, and helped me see my own challenges from a new perspective. The recommendation to read it with colleagues really could not have been more true for me —At our next staff meeting, I brought up how great of a read it was and that our team should review it together. There were even a few passages I marked to show colleagues because it echoed conversations we recently had."

Kristine Bogue, M.S.
Director of Student Compliance/Deputy Title IX Coordinator
Jefferson College

"As a 30+ year educator, this book, *Beginning Within: Marking a New Journey Toward Equity in Trauma-Informed Education Practices,* reinforced many of the challenges and issues that I have faced in the educational world. It offers a powerful lens into the intersection of trauma, equity, and systemic change in education. Grounded in the voices and experiences of a variety of authors, its reflections are both personal and practical, honoring lived experiences while offering pathways for transformation. It reminded me why I became a teacher in the first place: to help create a safe, just, and empowering space for *all* students. This is essential reading for any educator committed to trauma-informed educational practices seeking organizational change."

Dr. Mollie Bolton
Chief of Teaching, Learning & Accountability
Special School District of St. Louis County

"With a poignant urgency evident in this compendium, readers will gain the authors' collective wisdom of the complexity of childhood trauma and an evidence-based, yet relatable, framework for responding. Perspectives on trauma ingrained in self-care, to trauma rooted in children's communities, to trauma present on university and systemic levels are woven seamlessly together, giving readers both an empirical and deeply humane understanding of being trauma informed. Anyone that supports students will identify with this book's insight and will feel compelled to act."

Jennifer Heithaus, MD
Associate Professor
Director, Division of Developmental Pediatrics
Fellowship Director, Developmental-Behavioral Pediatrics
Department of Pediatrics
Saint Louis University School of Medicine

"The impact of trauma is seen in every school building across the United States. The authors of *Beginning Within: Marking a New Journey Toward Equity in Trauma-Informed Education Practices* share research and personal experiences regarding equity, safety and organizational change. This is a recommended read for educators who want to gain a new perspective on practices within their work, including students across all levels, so they may foster healing, growth and ultimately, the ability to thrive."

Dr. Deanne McCullough
Director of Trauma-Informed Programs
Missouri Baptist University
St. Louis MO

"From an educator's perspective, this book is as relevant as it gets. We are not only teaching reading and math but educating our students in how to manage life. From a behaviorist's perspective, it highlights the dynamic shift in how we define and address behavior in the classroom. What used to be a straightforward assignment of behavioral function to one of four categories (tangible, sensory, attention, escape) is now a complex web of experiences and emotions that changes how we mediate behaviors. The practical applications provided in this book are essential tools for all educators and behavior analysts in today's culture and are paving the way for all schools to become truly trauma-informed."

Christea Reiser, Ed.S., BCBA
Hillsboro RIII School District
Hillsboro MO

"*Beginning Within: Marking a New Journey Toward Equity in Trauma Informed Education Practices* is a groundbreaking text that moves the education field into the forefront of best practice. This text provides exceptional insight for teachers, administrators, education students, and their partners, including mental health professionals and students on the movement of trauma-informed education. As society moves through the post-COVID era, the authors consider the impact of the pandemic on students and faculty, as well as adverse childhood events and community violence. Their trauma-informed approach of taking a lived experience perspective at every level, from elementary school through college, maintains the reader's emotional involvement, making this text unique in two ways. The reader can connect to genuine examples of teachers and students who have experienced different types of trauma and adverse childhood events, learning from first-hand examples the importance of trauma-informed education. These examples from classroom practice also demonstrate key tenets of trauma-informed care, establishing that the authors are truly living what they are exploring and explaining, helping the reader see that trauma-informed education is not a buzzword but a way-of-life, essential for today's schools. While lived examples are an emotion-evoking core component of the text, key theories are pulled through with research to prove the grounding and validity of the need for equitable, trauma-informed models described throughout the text. As one of the contributors to the Missouri Model of Trauma-Informed Care and a former social work professor, I highly endorse *Beginning Within* as a primary text for trauma-informed education."

Heidi Strickler, PhD, LCSW-S,
CEDS-C, CART, CTLS

BEGINNING WITHIN

Myers Education Press

Published by Myers Education Press, LLC
P.O. Box 424
Gorham, ME 04038

Myers Education Press is an academic publisher specializing in books, e-books, and digital content in the field of education. All of our books are subjected to a rigorous peer review process and produced in compliance with the standards of the Council on Library and Information Resources.

Library of Congress Cataloging-in-Publication Data available from Library of Congress.

13-digit ISBN 978-1-9755-0638-4 (paperback)
13-digit ISBN 978-1-9755-0639-1 (library networkable e-edition)
13-digit ISBN 978-1-9755-0640-7 (consumer e-edition)

Printed in the United States of America.
All first editions printed on acid-free paper that meets the American National Standards Institute Z39-48 standard.

Cover design by Teresa Lagrange

BEGINNING WITHIN

Marking a New Journey Toward Equity in Trauma-Informed Education Practices

EDITED BY
JOANNE C. FISH
AND JAMIE DORONKIN

Myers Education Press
Gorham, Maine

CONTENTS

Foreword

Mark LaCelle-Peterson
President and CEO
Association for Advancing Quality in Educator Preparation (AAQEP)

LIFE IN SCHOOLS AND classrooms is increasingly challenging, in large part because the lives of children and families are increasingly challenging. In conversations with teachers across the country during the COVID-19 pandemic and in its aftermath, trauma's impact on students, families, and educators has been a central and urgent concern. Of course, the alarm bells were ringing long before COVID hit, warning us of the impact of adverse childhood experiences (ACEs) and adverse community environments (the other ACEs) on students and their families. However, the pandemic and its aftermath brought increasing awareness and urgency to the conversation about trauma-informed approaches to education as the impact of adverse experiences and environments on children, young people, families, and communities became increasingly evident in daily classroom life, creating secondary traumatic impacts for students and teachers. Increasing numbers of students exhibited disruptive behaviors, difficulty in focusing on academic tasks, and inability to interact socially with peers or adults. Teachers expressed frustration, exhaustion, and discouragement, often despairing at their inability to support individuals impacted by adversity or to maintain stable learning environments for all.

Fortunately, over the years, a solid body of research and practice has emerged to provide educators with an understanding not only of the impacts of the two ACEs, but also of the neurological and behavioral dynamics caused by trauma-induced stressors. Those understandings can support trauma-informed approaches to intervention and education. While no intervention can remove or reverse the initial adversity, appropriate interventions can provide a way forward to safe and productive learning environments in the short run, and in the best cases, to growth and healing in the long run. This book is a timely and comprehensive support for educators at all levels who deal with trauma's negative effects and seek to foster such growth and healing.

One commonly heard qualification about trauma-informed approaches in education bears repeating: There are no shortcuts and no silver bullets, no ready-to-serve trauma-informed techniques, and no scripted curriculum or pacing guide for caring. But there are trauma-sensitive, informed, and responsive practitioners and leaders. Indeed, trauma-informed practices are not a set of techniques to be 'implemented with fidelity' in order to 'solve the problem of trauma.' The focus, in other words, is not on 'practices' but rather on 'informed.' Teachers who have developed effective approaches to serving trauma-impacted students and families report that the key to ameliorating trauma's impact in the classroom is not a set of discrete *new practices* but a *new perspective.* What makes the difference is a 'lens' for viewing student behaviors and understanding the origins of students' stress and anxiety, for identifying triggering factors that set off defensive behaviors, that shut down communication. Their informed professional response—their educational practices—drew on the existing practical expertise, informed by a deeper understanding of students' experiences, past and in the moment. Crucially, trauma-informed perspectives and responses allow learners to be supported in the classroom itself. While collaboration with fellow professionals who can address root causes and provide targeted support is of immense value, learners must be able to thrive in the classroom—trauma-informed solutions benefit from collaboration but should not require 'outsourcing.'

In considering the current need for trauma-informed perspectives, it is also prudent, unfortunately, to acknowledge that educational settings themselves can be sources of toxic stress for students and for adults. Prior to the pandemic experience, education had, for the better part of two decades, been shaped by a set of policies and directives that prioritized academic performance in select subjects at the expense of other subjects and, crucially, at the expense of a holistic approach to student well-being. One consequence of this narrowed conception of students and schooling was that during and in the aftermath of the COVID-19 pandemic's social and educational disruptions, schools were somewhat out of practice in addressing the whole individual—a key aspect of trauma-informed approaches. This is not meant as a criticism of teachers or schools or to imply that empathetic and holistic approaches were altogether absent from all schools and classrooms. Nonetheless, the focus of schools, and sadly, even the responses of some education leaders and policymakers, have often been alarm over 'learning loss' itself rather than over the continuing traumatic experiences of which it is a symptom. Our focus as educators—at the classroom, school, district, and policy levels—must be on ensuring students' well-being, sense of safety, and ability to thrive. The chapters in this volume provide support and guidance for educators in each of these locations.

In fact, the chapters in this book admirably address the importance and potential of all educators, regardless of role or position within the system to support learners and families experiencing the impact of trauma—from classrooms where all can thrive while the worst-wounded find solace, to state policies developed through wide collaboration. The book you are about to read is solidly grounded in relevant theories from a number of disciplines and perspectives. It is filled with examples of effective efforts to address the impact of trauma at every level of the school system and across the educational ecosystem, from educator preparation to policy-making. At the system level, it includes an account of how human service providers, including educators, came together across the state of Missouri to create frameworks and implementation guides. It is a valuable case study in policymaking that addresses both the impact of adverse childhood experiences and adverse community environments and engages professionals from many agencies in a coordinated and systemic effort. It also includes accounts of classroom educators who have combined their insights into the effects of the two ACEs with their own expertise as practitioners to create safe spaces that are responsive to students' needs rather than practices that are reactive to particular classroom incidents.

The authors and editors of this volume have done a great service to the field by demystifying the approach to successfully addressing the impact of trauma in classrooms and schools and by providing concrete proofs of concept across the levels of schooling and throughout the educational ecosystem. I would recommend reading it together with colleagues: Creating communities of trauma-informed professionals can provide us all with care and support as we create educational contexts where all students can thrive.

Acknowledgments

To Jamie—who always kept the process moving along and taught me so much about checking in with myself.

There is no doubt that life is better when it's shared. When I first thought about this book project, I knew I needed the knowledge and wisdom of others who had experience in various facets of trauma-informed practices. The first person I thought of was my co-editor, Jamie Doronkin. She and I have been working together since 2013, and we went to our first training on trauma-informed practices together. I could not have asked for a better writing and editing partner.

This book would not have been possible without Jamie. Our weekly book meetings, our work lunches, and our shared OneDrive collaborations have been inspiring and motivating. Her quiet wisdom and calmness kept me sane throughout this process, even in the midst of the upheaval of both of our careers, job changes, and an open-heart surgery. I might have started this process, but this book would never have made it to the publisher had it not been for her. Ours is a friendship I will always cherish, and I can't wait until our next collaboration!

—Joanne Fish

To Joanne—

I have so appreciated your consistent courage in this project, especially when I questioned whether we could meet the deadline for this book. This has been such an easy collaboration with you, and I have marveled many times about how similar our thoughts and beliefs were as we coordinated the design and structure of this book and composed our shared chapters. I, too, look forward to more work together and wonder what courageous collaborations you may steer us toward next!

In appreciation of our great friendship and our equally great professional collaborations!

—Jamie Doronkin

To our chapter authors—thank you for your authenticity and your dedication and for sharing your expertise in your chapters—your work is what made this book come to life.

Introduction

THE CHAPTERS IN THIS book were written and edited as the tenth anniversary of Michael Brown's shooting befell, reminding all of us about the young Black man who was shot and killed by a white police officer in Ferguson, Missouri, in August 2014. There is no doubt that this was a tragedy for all of the parties involved. The first chapter anchors this book by sharing developments from the Ferguson Commission, appointed by the Missouri Governor via Executive Order after Michael Brown's shooting, to investigate issues around equality and safety. The first chapter also shares the response of the St. Louis Regional Health Commission and other community agencies and foundations that have been working since 2014 to help create a greater understanding of the impact of trauma and toxic stress on the well-being of communities and their constituents.

It is unfortunate that it took a traumatic event such as this for an investigation to be commissioned that would reveal the inequities and inadequacies found within the labyrinthian system of mechanisms that regulate our public service organizations. The Ferguson Commission's findings highlighted the necessity for schools to understand the impact of childhood trauma (including poverty and personal and community trauma) on students' behavior and learning. The Ferguson Commission's report called for the creation of "trauma-informed schools and districts" (The Ferguson Commission Report, 2015, p. 115). The report stated that it is important to "ensure evidence-based trauma-informed training and support is offered to families, teachers and students" (p. 115). The report prioritized finding out *why* trauma was happening and *what* needed to happen in order to help those who lived within its grasp. This book is an effort to traverse the labyrinth of factors that impact students' and educators' work of learning and teaching in the midst of experiencing trauma and toxic stress. We hope this work will help them grow and maybe even thrive.

What This Book Offers

The chapters in this book reflect the growth, grief, and galvanizing challenges that have shaped and continue to shape our understanding of equality, safety, and organizational change around trauma-informed educational practices. Our nation's history has repeatedly informed us that change can be both exciting and traumatic, and organizational change is no exception (Kotter, 1996/2012). We also know that change efforts can stall without a sense of safety and support as part of the culture of change (Harris & Fallot, 2001).

This book is a culmination of research, contemplations, and ideas that address some of the lesser-discussed concepts around trauma-informed practices in education. When inviting authors to share their wisdom, we asked them to consider the following frameworks:

> **John Kotter's (1996/2012)** ***Eight-Step Model for Organizational Change*****:** (1) establishing a sense of urgency; (2) creating the guiding coalition; (3) developing a vision and strategy; (4) communicating the change vision; (5) empowering for broad-based action; (6) generating short-term wins; (7) consolidating gains and producing more change; (8) anchoring new approaches in the culture.

> **Fallot and Harris' (2001)** ***Five Guiding Principles of Trauma-Informed Practice*****:** (1) safety; (2) trustworthiness; (3) choice; (4) collaboration; and (5) empowerment.

> **Smith et al.'s, (2017) five-level** ***Building Equity Taxonomy*** that includes: (1) physical integration; (2) social-emotional engagement; (3) opportunity to learn; (4) instructional excellence; and (5) engaged and inspired learners.

Our authors have chosen to embrace some lesser-researched and discussed topics around trauma-informed practices (which is why we invited them to contribute to this book). We wanted to be sure organic voices were represented. Some of these include: hearing from teachers who tell us about the barriers they face when attempting to implement trauma-informed practices; reading quotes from college students who were reflecting on their adolescent experiences around trauma and toxic stress responses, and hearing directly from elementary students who explain why they acted out in their class when they became frustrated or angry.

The first chapter explains how systems theory can inform our thinking around establishing a culture of trauma-informed practices. Schools and school districts are not truly trauma-informed unless they have created a *culture* of being such.

Several chapters talk about the concept of *urgency*. However, this concept is viewed in two completely different ways. One is in a more negative light: We have created a culture of urgency that causes us to ignore our own needs. Teachers are pushed into this with expectations of getting through all the curriculum, making pedagogical changes on the whim of state legislators, attending to students' needs immediately, and making sure everything is graded in a timely manner. ... It never seems to stop. Taking care of oneself is generally pushed aside and never included in that urgency realm. On the other hand, John Kotter's framework for change (1996/2012) mentions creating a sense of urgency, which is important to get buy-in from those key players in an organization looking for change. This is a different type of urgency that is explained in a variety of places throughout this book.

Not all the chapters discuss K–12 contexts. One chapter discusses the importance of attending to the needs of college students and how peer-to-peer collaboration may be an answer to the ever-pressing need to help college students address mental health needs. This chapter is part of a section on implementing trauma-informed practices that also addresses the barriers teachers experience when attempting to practice what they have been trained to do. Our chapter on allowing choices highlights the importance of empowering middle school students by creating space in their day for making those choices. Another chapter helps us think about ways to create equity among secondary students who have experienced trauma. We also offer some thoughts on the importance of considering belonging as a way to bring all these concepts together.

Organizational Improvement Ideas

In the last chapter, we offer a number of organizational improvement ideas that readers can take with them into the field of education. Whether the reader is a pre-service teacher, a current teacher, an aspiring or current administrator, or an educator preparation faculty member, we hope they will consider the ideas we offer and take what might work within their own schools or academic organizations.

The Cambridge online dictionary defines an organization as "a group whose members work together for a shared purpose in a continuing way" (Cambridge dictionary, n.d.). The shared purpose, we argue, is that schools work to provide high-quality education to students. This may sound a bit vague. The truth is, different groups define high-quality education differently. To some, it may be to prepare students for college or career readiness. To others, it may be to prepare students for a life in which they can pursue their own passions, be well-rounded and productive citizens, and be committed to living honest lives with social justice. Frankly, we should consider the purpose of education from the perspectives of the students themselves. Regardless of the stated purpose, The Ferguson Commission's report mentions the word *school* 511 times (including references). This is indicative of the importance of schools as organizations in the work of mitigating trauma in the lives of students.

As organizational change evolves around creating, engaging, and implementing trauma-informed education practice, the need for equity also abounds—equity that supports success and is built on the needs of those impacted by the change (Smith et al., 2017). Identifying needs and experiencing safety, support, and equity are paramount for those in school organizations undergoing change; otherwise, the opportunity for stirring up more trauma is heightened (Venet, 2021). Here's to stirring up change instead by *beginning within and* marking a new journey toward equity in trauma-informed education practices.

References

Cambridge Dictionary. (n.d.) Organization. In Cambridge dictionary. https://dictionary.cambridge.org/dictionary/english/organization.

Exec. Order No. 14-15. S.O.S.C.D. (November 18, 2014).

Ferguson Commission Report. (2015). *Forward through Ferguson: A path toward racial equity.*

Harris, M. & Fallot, R. (Eds.) (2001). *Using trauma theory to design service systems: New directions for mental health services.* Jossey-Bass.

Kotter, J. P. (1996). *Leading change.* Harvard Business School Press.

Kotter, J. P. (2012). *Leading change: With a new preface by the author.* Harvard Business School Press.

Smith, D., Frey N., Pumpian, I., & Fisher, D. (2017). *Building equity: Policies and practices to empower all learners.* ASCD.

Venet, A. S. (2021). *Equity-centered trauma-informed education.* W. W. Norton and Company.

CHAPTER 1

Systems Theory—Embedding the Culture of Trauma-Informed Education:

Reviewing a Decade of Work Since the August 2014 Ferguson Missouri Shooting

PATRICIA CARTER AND JENNIFER BRINKMANN

An Unflinching Investigation

IN AUGUST 2014, IN Ferguson, Missouri, a suburb of St. Louis, a young Black man, Michael Brown, was shot and killed by a white police officer. After months of protest and civil unrest, the governor of Missouri appointed the Ferguson Commission "to conduct a thorough, wide-ranging and unflinching study of the social and economic conditions that impede progress, equality and safety in the St. Louis region" (Exec. Order No. 14–15, 2014, para. 2). The report from the Ferguson Commission (2015) prioritized child well-being and highlighted data that showed that school discipline is not distributed equally: In the 2011–2012 school year, 14.3% of Black elementary school students in Missouri were suspended, compared to 1.8% of white students. Missouri's discipline gap between Black students and White students was the largest among the 48 states studied (Losen et al., 2015). In addition to hurting academic performance, this disproportionate discipline of Black students lowers teacher expectations and has been shown to increase the likelihood of future incarceration (Okonofua & Eberhardt, 2015). Simultaneously, the St. Louis Regional Health Commission responded to community feedback and launched a campaign, Alive and Well STL, to create an understanding of the impact of trauma and toxic stress on well-being.

The Missouri (MO) Model for Trauma-Informed Schools

Schools in the St. Louis area began to experience political pressure to act. The St. Louis Regional Health Commission, with the support of the Missouri Foundation for Health and the leadership of the Missouri Trauma Roundtable (2015), sponsored by the state, developed a pilot for schools and districts in the region that wanted to become *trauma-informed*. The Missouri Model: A Developmental Framework for Trauma Informed Schools was used as the guide. With the completion of the pilot, a group of education leaders emerged who were committed to working across the St. Louis region to advance educational equity using trauma-informed care as a model for implementation. One of these leaders, Sharonica Hardin-Bartley, PhD, had served on a working group of the Ferguson Commission and had recently been appointed superintendent of the School District of University City. She chaired the working group through the local non-profit Alive and Well Communities, created after the Alive and Well STL campaign. This non-profit facilitated the creation of the Missouri Model for Trauma-Informed Schools at the request of the state Trauma Roundtable, working with the education leaders in St. Louis. This network of partners weaved the insights from community members with the expertise of education leaders and the early adopters of trauma-informed care across the state to create the Missouri Model for Trauma-Informed Schools. Each part of the system played an integral role in adapting the original Missouri Model for the school environment.

Becoming a Community School of Choice

Since the development of the Missouri Model for Trauma-Informed Schools in 2018, Dr. Hardin-Bartley, who served on the Ferguson Commission and guided the development of the Missouri Model for Trauma-Informed Schools, has led the School District of University City through significant transformation. Through the district's "Learning Reimagined" initiative, the district has been focused on creating a new educational experience and school culture. The initiative focuses on social-emotional wellness, authentic and heartfelt relationships, racial equity, nurturing student voice and social action, increased measurement and continued improvement of school and student academic performance, and teacher support for leadership and improvement.

The superintendent and her colleagues of education leaders in the St. Louis region have been vocal advocates for the adoption of trauma-informed care and the prioritization of child and family well-being within the education system. They recognize that students can't learn when they are not well, and teachers can't teach when they are not well. As a result, in 2023, when public schools were struggling to maintain enrollment after the trauma of the COVID-19 pandemic, the School District of University City experienced increases in enrollment, making it a school district of choice for its community.

Why Focus on Trauma?

In 1998, Felitti et al., shared with the world their findings from what has become known as the Adverse Childhood Experiences (ACEs) study. This groundbreaking information identified the prevalence and long-term impact of trauma. Following this discovery, research focusing on trauma took two tracks: one that developed effective trauma-specific treatments and the other that delved into the neurological and biological pathways through which trauma can impact brain development.

Research on trauma's impact on the brain and body began identifying several factors that not only were critical to healing from trauma's impact but also were equally effective in helping children develop resilience to act as an arguably permeable shield from the negative impact of adverse childhood experiences. These concepts include the role of attachment, how our brain and body respond to fear and safety, as well as how the brain and body can become over- or under-sensitized to reminders of these experiences (Siegel, 2010).

Several terms began appearing in the literature, such as *trauma-specific* and trauma-informed. The term *trauma-specific* is typically applied to a clinical or other type of intervention to reflect that it is driven by an understanding of the impact of trauma and is designed to target the impact of trauma specifically. Some examples of evidence-based trauma-specific clinical interventions include Trauma-Focused Cognitive Behavioral Therapy (TF-CBT), Prolonged Exposure Therapy (PET), and Eye Movement Desensitization and Reprocessing (EMDR). Cognitive Behavioral Interventions for Trauma in Schools/CBITS (Jaycox et al., 2018) is a specific intervention applied in schools as well as Animating Learning by Integrating and Validating Experience/ALIVE (Frydman & Mayor, 2017).

Trauma-Informed Means a Shift in Culture

The term trauma-inform*ed* has been, and continues today, to be utilized and defined differently, along with being implemented with different foci and outcomes. This has led to a lack of agreement and accountability across systems and organizations, which poses challenges for those who have experienced trauma to genuinely access resources within a trauma-informed culture. Trauma-informed is not a specific intervention, service, or program; rather, it is a shift in an organization's culture driven by examining policies and practices and shifting views of environmental and relational factors. Often, the term is misapplied. For example, having professional development training on trauma's impact and then claiming to be trauma-informed or utilizing a trauma screening tool without comprehensive support and readiness is an incomplete response. If no actual policy or cultural changes are implemented, then it would seem trauma-informed is not effective. This lack of consensus on the term can also make efforts to study trauma-informed challenging (Maynard et al., 2019). Meta-analysis of research on trauma-informed schools found widespread variation in frameworks and semantics, with most focusing on what are referred to as interventions as opposed to research that focused on processes and innovations (Maynard et al., 2019). This limitation of research on interventions rather than the overall ethos of a school undermines the essence of being trauma-informed.

Like other systems, state education departments and schools began recognizing the impact trauma had on students' behavior and often looked to mental health partners to train educators on trauma and accept referrals to treat the students' trauma to reduce behavioral issues, essentially *outsourcing* responsibility for students with trauma to the mental health system. However, other schools and education systems have moved beyond behavioral issues to accept trauma's impact on students' ability to learn, independent of behavioral issues. This requires educators to go beyond making referrals to mental health services and examine their curriculum, policies, and environments through the trauma lens and recognize how being trauma-informed can help meet the schools' desired outcomes.

A Multi-Level Approach to Becoming Trauma-Informed

This chapter presents a multi-level approach by which the field of education can become trauma-informed, recognizing the interdependence of the different levels: state roles, community responses, and district and school responses. We also explore what each system level can do independently to support students who have experienced trauma and how those systems can help students build resilience to mitigate the impact of future trauma. We include Missouri's response in each of these areas as well.

State Roles

Four ways in which the state systems can support local implementation in schools include:

1. Convening and Championing
2. Building Consensus
3. Creating Incentives
4. Building Change Agents

Convening and Championing

The state, through various departments such as mental health, education, or social services, can be the voice that initially recognizes the impact trauma can have on its citizens and raise the issue across systems. A multi-system approach at the state level can create synergy and guidance that can be used at the community level. We know that trauma has the potential to impact almost all areas of a person's life, including educational, relational, financial, physical, and emotional health. The state, whether through a specific department/system or at the Governor's office level, can bring together all systems and champion the need to address trauma. In the case of schools, the state department of education can champion the need for schools and educators to learn about trauma and, through review of statewide policies, support schools in making the changes needed. One way to increase a systematic approach is for the state department of education to insist that educator preparation programs include trauma-informed pedagogies in their curricula.

A state-level interagency group can meet the needs of all citizens by recognizing that trauma can impact multiple areas of functioning, such as learning, mental and physical health, employment, and finance, as well as parenting, relationships, and community functioning. It also allows a lifespan approach. The intrinsic authority of this group needs to lie within its expertise; in other words, it must include actual practitioners in the respective fields, those with lived experience, as well as state administrators. The group must be knowledgeable of and driven by the growing science around trauma and ideally minimize any impact of social or political bias.

Missouri's Response to Convening and Championing

The authors of this chapter led and/or were of the team that made up the Missouri Trauma Roundtable. Although convened and facilitated by a state department, included on the Roundtable were those who had been doing innovative work in the field of trauma, whether with children or adults, and from prevention to provision of trauma-specific services. Those who had experienced trauma were also represented. This group was dedicated to increasing understanding of the prevalence and impact of trauma across all sectors and the lifespan. State organizations/agencies were invited to participate as they committed to promoting trauma-informed practices within their strategic plans and supported this with various innovations being implemented.

Building Consensus

As noted earlier, the term trauma-informed has yet to be clearly defined across our country, with even trauma champions using the term differently. Part of the variability is understanding that this is not solely a mental health issue. Recognizing trauma's impact in multiple and diverse areas of functioning creates a need for each system to take responsibility. When limited to behavioral health, addressing trauma can be reduced to a need for treatment without noting that other domains, such as schools, need to address trauma's impact not only on behavior but also on their ability to educate students whose ability to learn has been disrupted by trauma.

Without a clear consensus on a shared understanding of trauma-informed, it is difficult to support and hold organizations accountable and for consumers to know what to expect from an organization that identifies itself as trauma-informed. The state, through its interagency group, can review and develop or adapt a definition of trauma-informed that reflects a shared understanding and commitment.

The Substance Abuse and Mental Health Services Administration (SAMHSA) offered one of the first definitions of trauma-informed at the federal level in *A Treatment Improvement Protocol: Trauma-Informed Care in Behavioral Health Services* (2014), which stated that a program, organization, or system is trauma-informed when it:

A. Realizes the widespread impact of trauma and understands potential paths for healing;

B. Recognizes the signs and symptoms of trauma in staff, clients, and others involved with the system; and

C. Responds by fully integrating knowledge about trauma into policies, procedures, practices, and settings.

This definition involves viewing trauma through an ecological and cultural lens and recognizing that context plays a significant role in how individuals perceive and process traumatic events, whether acute (sudden and short-term) or chronic (gradual and long-term).

Although the SAMHSA definition was directed towards behavioral health organizations, it can and has been applied across several different entities, such as a treatment agency, school district, health clinic, library, or even across a community. Trauma-informed is not achieved through training or professional development alone, nor can it be accomplished within a short timeframe. Rather, it is a developmental process that scaffolds learnings and applications and requires intention and attention over years until it is fully integrated into the ethos of the entity and becomes the norm. By building consensus, a shared language is developed that can support widespread dissemination and uptake. Consensus also can help ensure quality.

As noted previously, some organizations will take one or two action steps, such as screening for trauma or having a trauma-specific intervention available, and then identify as trauma-informed when they are not. For example, many schools have had one to eight professional development hours on trauma, including information on prevalence, impact on brain development, signs, and evidence-based mental health interventions. Some may even have some training in skills to help calm a dysregulated student. The school administration feels they have done due diligence in being trauma-informed, although no policies have changed, no work has been done in supporting staff well-being, and there is no change in the school's environment/culture. Students and staff are still struggling with their sense of psychological and physical safety and feeling disengaged, and disciplinary issues continue to increase and focus on exclusionary practices. Having a consensus that trauma-informed is a cultural and ideational shift that goes beyond any one service can counter misguided claims and support quality implementation. By having a broad consensus on the breadth of trauma-informed, all systems can see their role and responsibilities.

Missouri's Response to Building Consensus

The Missouri Trauma Roundtable spent its first year exploring the meaning of trauma-informed, the breadth and depth of being trauma-informed, and what needed to be done to extend it beyond mental health (2015). The Roundtable members explored what it would mean to have a trauma-informed school (or a prison or even a library, church, store, or food pantry). Although it is not the responsibility of these agencies to treat trauma, given the populations served, it is their responsibility to recognize and mitigate trauma's impact as well as reduce the risk of retraumatizing individuals.

The Missouri Model: A Developmental Framework for Trauma-Informed Schools

The Missouri Model: A Developmental Framework for Trauma-Informed (https://cfechildwellbeing.org/resource/the-missouri-model-a-developmental-framework-for-trauma-informed/) was developed to create consensus across the state and was intentionally applicable across all systems and not just mental health. This consensus identified definitions, processes, and indicators to guide any organization on the journey to being trauma-informed. This required a facilitated discussion to identify and merge all systems' needs, challenge thinking and biases, and work through conflicts. Many early models of trauma-informed were dichotomous—an entity was trauma-informed, or it was not. Due to the enormity of work that being trauma-informed requires, it can seem overwhelming, so some organizations never start the journey. The Missouri Model: A Developmental Approach to Trauma-Informed (Missouri Department of Mental Health and Partners [MDMHP], 2014) was the first model to include a staged, or developmental, approach. This model utilized the components of the Fallot and Harris (2011) trauma-informed model and broke it down into four stages with definitions, processes, and indicators. The Missouri Model was developed by experts across various systems and organizations with a history of successfully addressing trauma through treatment or environmental interventions and includes four developmental phases (MDMHP, 2014).

Missouri Model's four phases of becoming trauma-informed

1. **Trauma-aware:** The focus is on learning about trauma and its impact to support a shift in knowledge and attitudes.

2. **Trauma Sensitive:** Focus on knowledge, application, and skill development.

3. **Trauma Responsive:** Focus on changing the organizational culture to respond to the impact of trauma on clients, staff, and stakeholders, including addressing structural inequities. At all levels of the organization, staff begin rethinking the routines and infrastructure of the organization and how this can impact client outcomes.

4. **Trauma-Informed:** The organization has made trauma-responsive and inclusive practices the organizational norm, and these practices are so embedded that they no longer depend on a few leaders. The organization intentionally seeks out diverse partners, including marginalized populations and people with lived experiences, to strengthen trauma-informed collaboration.

Creating Incentives

State-funded departments can support schools and other agencies in starting the journey to being trauma-informed and sustaining the change.

States have taken different approaches to moving schools toward being trauma-informed. One approach is to legislatively require schools to do the work. This approach ensures uptake, although not necessarily buy-in. It can be particularly challenging when local school boards do not have the understanding or resources to have the district do the work. If statewide resources are not directed to support the change financially, it becomes an unfunded mandate, usually resulting in fragmented implementation.

Another approach is to incentivize the uptake without mandates. This approach aligns more with the trauma-informed approach by avoiding an authoritarian mechanism and offering a collaborative process. The school or district can engage its board, families, students, and staff to reflect on outcomes and set priorities unique to its culture and population. Incentives at the state level can also include identifying indicators of being trauma-informed within the statewide assessments of schools.

Offering funding for implementation can incentivize schools to work towards becoming trauma-informed. If the school has the expertise, there are fewer costs, outside of staff time, to begin and sustain the process. In Missouri, funding was provided for agencies to begin the journey toward trauma-informed approaches. Through this, the state learned what it takes for an organization to do the work. The primary cost was for the external national trauma expert and consultant; however, mini-grants were also provided to support the implementation of some components.

Missouri's Response to Creating Incentives

All resources developed by the Trauma Roundtable were openly shared across systems and were reviewed and adapted for use in other states. When Missouri passed legislation requiring schools to have information about trauma on their websites, the Roundtable provided the Missouri Model (MDMHP, 2014) and the Missouri Model for Trauma-Informed Schools (Alive and Well Communities Educational Leader's Workgroup, 2019) to post on the education department's website for schools for easy access. Training videos on trauma and being trauma-informed were provided to the state Medicaid agency in support of a specialized managed care contract for youth in state custody. Schools could obtain free initial training on trauma and with follow-up, could access trainers and consultants to support the journey towards trauma-informed. With the onset of the COVID-19 pandemic, the state Department of Education was able to reach out to organizations that were members of the Trauma Roundtable to access webinars and videos to support schools and students. Other examples of incentives that indirectly impacted education included providing an enhanced rate for trauma-specific therapies for children and youth and allowing schools to bill Medicaid without having to make the match for therapy services for non-special education students. Additionally, the Roundtable was able to advocate for the inclusion of occupational therapists as behavioral health providers for Medicaid billing due to the growing focus on sensory and somatic interventions to address trauma.

Building Change Agents

Any type of change can be difficult to accept and manage. Change can often take away our sense of mastery as we learn new skills. It is important, then, to intentionally focus on the management of change in the form of a paradigm shift. As noted previously, being trauma-informed goes well beyond professional development hours on trauma. It is a multi-year initiative that focuses on changing the organization's culture. It requires us to revise our underlying assumptions and shift priorities. It includes a review of existing policies and practices through the lens of trauma and revising as needed. It also goes beyond just changing policy; it must support the implementation of new policies. For example, simply stating that students will not be suspended in elementary school does not provide educators the knowledge, skills, and tools to effectively address student behavior, leaving staff frustrated and reducing the impact of the revised policies.

To support change work, the state can provide guidance on the process of becoming trauma-informed and the actual components of making and sustaining change. The change process and its impact must be identified and addressed. Several change management models can be used (Kotter et al., 2021; Lewin, 1947; Walton & Deming, 1988). All these models offer phases or specific strategic components. States are often not attuned to the requirements for such change and instead want quick changes that can occur in a legislative cycle with concrete outcomes quickly available. The state must commit to and support the time process of real change. The state must continue to monitor the barriers to making and sustaining change in schools working to be trauma-informed and offer guidance and supports.

The state's expectations for change should be aligned with these models, noting that the preliminary focus is on building understanding and consensus. State-monitored goals and objectives reflect the process and initial preparatory steps and embrace the evolutionary nature of this work. As with the Missouri Model (MDMHP, 2014) and the Missouri Model for Trauma-Informed Schools (Alive and Well Communities Educational Leader's Workgroup, 2019), monitoring should be focused on phases of development that can wax and wane in response to external factors.

The state must be attuned to the growing science in different areas, such as brain development, physiological impact, and new and developing interventions. Similarly, the state should stay attuned to the variety of areas that intersect with the knowledge of trauma and resilience. The state itself must maintain fidelity to trauma-informed practices. Resources, politics, funding, and priorities can change quickly. Realistically, there may be barriers or even times when moving forward is challenging. The state must stay true to the model and openly identify when fidelity is challenged. Rather than dilute the model, it is important that the state find alternatives, such as pausing implementation, and recognize that it is better to take small steps towards the goal than give up.

Missouri's Response to Building Change Agents

The Missouri Model (MDMHD, 2014) and the Missouri Model for Trauma-Informed Schools (Missouri Department of Elementary, 2019) were specifically developed to create a map of the journey organizations can follow to become trauma-informed to assist in managing the change. They were the first trauma-informed models that recognized the developmental nature of this work rather than it being a dichotomous state of trauma-informed or not. The Missouri Trauma Roundtable (2015) also monitored uptake across the state and identified barriers. Roundtable members would discuss where they had been successful in different systems' uptake of the concept, with organizations taking actionable steps. For example, it was noted that many organizations were implementing screening for trauma as a first step and claiming to be trauma-informed. The Trauma Roundtable developed and made available a guidance document on implementing screening for trauma, noting the questions that needed to be asked and explored to develop a trauma-informed process before screening is implemented (Policy

Guidance On Screening For Trauma · Center For Child Well-Being). In the Missouri Model (MDMHP, 2014) and the Missouri Model for Trauma-Informed Schools (Missouri Department of Elementary, 2019), initiating screening is not an early step; rather, it is not implemented until the third phase of the model. (The Missouri Model for Trauma-Informed Schools [2019] can be accessed at: https://dmh.mo.gov/media/pdf/missouri-model-trauma-informed-schools). Another example was noting that schools were reluctant to begin this journey, so the Roundtable had a specific school guidance document developed in 2015. The Missouri Model for Trauma-Informed Schools' other guidance documents which are focused on human resources, leadership and organizational change, and community development through the public health model are available at https://cfechildwellbeing.org/resources/.

An internal barrier identified by the Missouri Trauma Roundtable (2015) was recognizing a growing tension between the early clinical approach focusing on adverse childhood experiences such as abuse and the growing focus on cultural or racial trauma and social determinants of health-related to diversity, equity, and inclusion (DEI). As the field of trauma-informed care has been developing, so has the field of DEI. Experts in these fields recognize each field as complementary to each other and necessary for both to succeed. However, school districts and other organizations struggle to simultaneously implement both fields' work. In some districts, this has resulted in districts choosing to focus on trauma *or* DEI.

In practice, neither trauma-informed care nor DEI alone can lead to healthy, equitable schools. Addressing trauma without acknowledging the harm of the trauma of racism, homophobia, transphobia, xenophobia, sexism, and other roots of oppression can further harm community members who have been marginalized and traumatized by discrimination. Furthermore, DEI work that seeks to add more staff diversity and improve outcomes for students with identities different from the majority can achieve true inclusion and belonging only when the trauma these individuals have experienced is acknowledged and understood.

The Missouri Trauma Roundtable (2015) addressed this tension by taking three steps requiring a top-down and bottom-up approach. First, the Trauma Roundtable needed to explore how the concepts of trauma-informed and DEI were related. A consensus was reached that without DEI, it is not possible to be truly trauma-informed. The next step was to adapt the trauma-informed principles initially adopted from the Fallot and Harris trauma-informed model (2011). This process included several local agencies and stakeholder groups exploring how the principles intersected and were defined by the concepts of DEI. The Trauma Roundtable then vetted the revised principles and disseminated them to guide the implementation of the DEI strategies and indicators. Next, through an extensive review and revision of the *Missouri Model* in 2019, DEI concepts and requirements were integrated into definitions, processes, and indicators while maintaining the continuum and providing a broad focus across all systems. These revised principles follow.

The Missouri Model: Five Key Principles of Trauma-Informed Care

The *Missouri Model* (Missouri Department of Mental Health, 2014) and the *Missouri Model for Trauma-Informed Schools* (Missouri Department of Elementary, 2019) are guided by five key principles: safety, trustworthiness, choice, collaboration, and empowerment. These principles are defined as the following:

Safety: Ensure physical and emotional safety, recognizing and responding to how racial, ethnic, religious, gender, or sexual identity may impact safety across the lifespan.

Trustworthiness: Foster genuine relationships and practices that build trust, making tasks clear, maintaining appropriate boundaries, and creating norms for interaction that promote reconciliation and healing. Understand and respond to how explicit and implicit power can affect the development of trusting relationships. This includes acknowledging and mitigating internal biases and recognizing the historic power of majority populations.

Choice: Maximize choice, addressing how privilege, power, and historic relationships impact both perceptions about and ability to act upon choice.

Collaboration: Honor transparency and self-determination and seek to minimize the impact of the inherent power differential while maximizing collaboration and sharing responsibility for making meaningful decisions.

Empowerment: Encouraging self-efficacy, identifying strengths, and building skills that lead to individual pathways for healing while recognizing and responding to the impact of historical trauma and oppression.

Community Response

As states have developed and led efforts to implement trauma-informed care, local communities have identified a variety of concerns that trauma-informed practices can help address. In some communities, leaders are concerned about poor educational and health outcomes, recognizing these poor outcomes often exist in the same zip codes that have experienced disinvestment, including the historic practice of redlining (Bradford et al., 2023). In some communities, residents have come to understand that students of color and students with disabilities often experience higher rates of expulsion and other punitive measures than do other students, which can lead to investigation by the federal Office of Civil Rights (Alaníz, 2024).

In some cases, when schools in these areas of disinvestment also experience action by the state, such as losing their accreditation, community members begin to demand accountability from the local schools for a better education for their children. Community members are motivated to advocate for high-quality schools because of the inextricable link between the quality of schools and property values. In school districts where a large portion of students live in poverty, families experience high levels of stress, which can often lead to high levels of dysregulation among students and behavior challenges in the classrooms, making it more difficult for educators to teach. And with the rise of the youth mental health crisis, school districts that often are isolated from other challenges because of their affluence often turn to trauma-informed care after their community experiences the loss of life from suicide (Agerbo et al., 2001).

As communities build new levels of awareness and understanding about why these outcomes exist, community members can rally to create the case for change. As community members become clear about the need for new approaches, they can begin to advocate for the change they want to see in their schools. Trauma-informed care provides a common framework for community members, parents, elected board members, educators, and students to work through solutions that prioritize the well-being of all.

The Pair of ACEs—Adverse Community Environments and Adverse Childhood Experiences

Research that followed the seminal Adverse Childhood Experiences study has provided an additional understanding of how adversity of all types impacts individual and population-level outcomes. Ellis and Dietz (2017) introduced the field to the *Pair of ACEs* framework, advocating for treating Adverse Community Environments (poverty, discrimination, community disruption, lack of opportunity, economic mobility, and social capital, poor housing quality and affordability, and violence) to prevent Adverse Childhood Experiences (domestic violence, substance abuse, emotional and sexual abuse, maternal depression, physical and emotional neglect, divorce, mental illness, incarceration, and homelessness). As state surveillance of adverse childhood experiences has grown, the evidence is clear that Black and Hispanic, non-White populations experience higher levels of ACEs than do other populations (Mersky et al., 2021). Without adding an understanding of the correlation of adverse community environments to adverse childhood experiences, researchers and practitioners risk drawing harmful conclusions about those who experience higher rates of adversity.

For example, some may say that the lack of fathers in the households contributes to higher rates of trauma. Using the Pair of ACEs framework, questions about why fathers may not be involved in family life can be better understood and addressed. When engaging community members in these conversations, new answers begin to emerge. For instance, fathers may not be involved because of higher rates of policing and incarceration, less access to jobs in their neighborhoods, and state benefits that disadvantage fathers. These insights can lead to new solutions: perhaps a school can offer employment for fathers. Some schools, for example, have created full-time positions for community members by combining several typical part-time roles, such as janitorial, food service, and transportation staff, giving families more financial security.

The Pair of ACEs research also aligns with the research that has identified and prioritized the treatment of the social determinants of health, defined by Healthy People 2030 as the "conditions in the environments where people are born, live, learn, work, play worship, and age that affect a wide range of health, functioning, and quality-of-life outcomes and risks" (Healthy People 2030, n.d.). Some determinants of health are protective, and some are harmful. For example, income can be predictive of long-term health. According to information shared by the American Public Health Association (APHA) by Krisberg (2016), the richest 1% of Americans can expect to live as many as 14 years longer than the poorest 1% of Americans. Housing can also influence health; for example, homes with lead can negatively impact childhood development because of lead poisoning. Other harmful factors in a home can cause uncontrolled asthma, which impacts school attendance. Education in and of itself can be a protective factor. According to the APHA, people who graduate from college live at least five years longer than those who don't finish high school (Krisberg, 2016).

District and School Response

When schools have the resources and support from their state and local communities, they explore implementation. Without a guide like the *Missouri Model for Trauma-Informed Schools* (Missouri Department of Elementary, 2019), schools often conduct a training and then struggle to determine their next steps. The initial trainings typically introduce educators to the Adverse Childhood Experiences study and the subsequent brain research, which provides educators with examples of how to support the regulation of student emotions. Still, they do not provide guidance on how schools/school districts can implement systemic change.

The Missouri Model for Trauma-Informed Schools (Alive and Well Communities Educational Leader's Workgroup, 2019) provides a wide range of indicators to guide schools in developing a cultural transformation that moves beyond implementing a training or a new curriculum. As schools have used this model, a few factors have emerged as keys to success where schools move beyond merely offering professional development on trauma (initial Trauma Awareness Phase):

1. Trauma teams comprising a diversity of individuals from the school community need to be given the time to meet regularly and with a small budget to implement programming.

2. Building leadership must be part of the trauma team. Even if the principal is unable to participate in all the meetings, leaders need to demonstrate their support for the initiative as a priority. Otherwise, meetings are canceled, work stalls, and it eventually stops altogether.

3. Leadership needs to recognize the initiative as a culture initiative rather than another program, creating expectations for staff that this is about changing mindsets and not adopting another curriculum.

4. Leadership that prioritizes staff well-being will build momentum for change and buy-in from teachers and others. Otherwise, teachers feel as though they are being asked to do one more thing without additional support. When teachers see shifts in their mindsets about their well-being, they are more likely to shift their mindsets for their students.

5. When trauma teams include caregivers (or students in older grades), progress often occurs faster. Because these individuals often experience trauma at the hands of the district, they can give voice to solutions and approaches that may not be evident to staff.

6. When district leadership models trauma-informed care, building leadership can better lead the change in their own buildings.

Conclusion

In summary, the state's role in the four areas of convening/championing, building consensus, creating and sustaining incentives, and being a change agent, is critical to support systems, communities, and organizations, including schools, to do the work of transforming cultures. By taking a leadership role, the state can build a comprehensive and integrated approach that connects different systems, communities, and organizations. Without state leadership, it is difficult, although not impossible, for communities, organizations, and even individuals to become trauma-informed. Progress and achievements can happen for those entities in states where a leadership role is not provided. A community can create its own consensus and add incentives, or a school leader can provide direction and resources. Similarly, a teacher can revise their approach to teaching, understand how trauma impacts students' learning and behavior, and alter their relationships and classroom environment. Ultimately, each level has a different sphere of influence. Work can go on in isolation at any level; however, the ultimate goal is to have children and families living, learning, and working in consistently supportive settings integrated across and throughout systems. When state systems provide support and resources for trauma-informed care, communities provide the will and support for change, and school leadership prioritizes implementation, trauma-informed schools are most likely to flourish and reach their potential.

However, in many cases, individual schools and teachers are left to do their part by applying a trauma-informed mindset without the support of their district, community, or state. Educators who are not supported by their community, building, or district leadership risk burnout if they try to meet all the needs of their students. Educators can create realistic expectations for themselves, including being a source of predictability for their students, modeling healthy relationships, communicating with students and other staff, and demonstrating care and concern for the students and families. Educators, like mental health clinicians, can benefit from having their own system of care to mitigate the impact of vicarious exposure to trauma. This can include formal therapy, informal support from like-minded educators, and a realistic, customized self-care plan.

References

Alive and Well Communities Educational Leader's Workgroup (2019). [Missouri model for trauma-informed schools]. Missouri Trauma Roundtable. https://dmh.mo.gov/sites/dmh/files/media/pdf/2019/05/missouri-model-trauma-informed-schools.pdf

Agerbo, E., Mortensen, P. B., Eriksson, T., Qin, P., & Westergaard-Nielson, N. (2001). Risk of suicide in relation to income level in people admitted to hospital with mental illness: A nested case-control study. https://doi.org/10.1136/bmj.322.7282.334

Alaníz, A. (2024). How youth of color with mental disabilities are excluded from school: A DisCrit and logistic regression analysis. *Child Abuse & Neglect, 158*, 107-144.

Bradford, J. M., Eldin, M. M., Golestani, S., Cardenas, T. C., Mery, M., Teixeira, P. G., DuBose, J., Brown, L. H., Bach, M., Robert, M. & Ali, S. (2023). Structural racism, residential segregation, and exposure to trauma: The persistent impact of redlining. *Journal of Trauma and Acute Care Surgery*, *97*(6), 891–894.

Ellis, W. & Dietz, W. (2017). A new framework for addressing adverse childhood and community experiences: The Building Community Resilience (BCR) model. *Academic Pediatrics 17*, S86-S93. https://doi.org/10.1016/j.acap.2016.12.011

Exec. Order No. 14-15. S.O.S.C.D. (November 18, 2014).

Fallot, R. D., & Harris, M. (2011). Creating cultures of trauma-informed care: Program self-assessment scale. *Community Connections*.

Felitti, V. J., Anda R. F., Nordenberg D., Williamson D. F., Spitz A. M., Edwards V., Koss M. P., & Marks J. S. (1998). Relationship of childhood abuse and household dysfunction to many of the leading causes of death in adults: The Adverse Childhood Experiences (ACE) study. *American Journal of Preventative Medicine 14*(4), 245–58. https://doi.org/10.1016/s0749-3797(98)00017-8

Ferguson Commission Report. (2015). *Forward through Ferguson: A path toward racial equity*. http://forwardthroughferguson.org

Frydman, J. S., & Mayor, C. (2017). Trauma and early adolescent development: Case examples from a trauma-informed public health middle school program. *Children and Schools, 39*(4), 238–247.

Healthy People (2030) (n.d.). Social determinants of health. Social Determinants of Health - Healthy People 2030. https://odphp.health.gov/healthypeople/priority-areas/social-determinants-health

Jaycox, L. H., Audra K. Langley, & Sharon A. H. (2018). *Cognitive behavioral intervention for trauma in schools (CBITS)* (2nd ed). RAND Corporation.

Kotter, J. P., Akhtar, V., & Gupta, G. (2021). *Change: How organizations achieve hard to imagine results in uncertain and volatile times*. John Wiley and Sons.

Krisberg, K. (2016). Income inequality: When wealth determines health: Earnings influential as lifelong social determinant of health. *The Nation's Health: A Publication of the American Public Health Association, 46*(8), 1–17.

Lewin K. (1947). Group decision and social change. In T. M. Newcomb, E. L. (Hartley (Eds.), *Readings in social psychology* (pp. 330–344). Henry Holt.

Losen, D., Hodson, C., Keith II, M. A., Morrison, K., & Belway, S. (2015). Are we closing the school discipline gap? University of California. Los Angeles. https://escholarship.org/uc/item/2t36g571#author

Maynard, B. R., Farina, A., Dell, N. A., & Kelly, M. S. (2019). Effects of trauma-informed approaches in schools: A systematic review. *Campbell Systematic Reviews, 15*(1–2).

Mersky, J. P., Choi, C., Plummer Lee, C., & Janczewski, C. E. (2021). Disparities in adverse childhood experiences by race/ethnicity, gender, and economic status: Intersectional analysis of a nationally representative sample. *Child abuse & neglect, 117*, Article 105066. https://doi.org/10.1016/j.chiabu.2021.105066

Missouri Department of Mental Health and Partners (2014). Missouri model: A developmental framework for trauma-informed approaches. https://dmh.mo.gov/media/pdf/missouri-model-developmental-framework-trauma-informed-approaches

Missouri Trauma Roundtable (2015). [Policy guidance on screening for trauma.] Missouri Department of Mental Health. https://dmh.mo.gov/sites/dmh/files/media/file/2019/01/mhc-meeting-screening-for-trauma-11122015.pdf

Okonofua, J. A., & Eberhardt, J. L. (2015). Two strikes: Race and the disciplining of young students. *Psychological science*, *26*(5), 617–624.

Siegel, D. J. (2010). *Mindsight: The new science of personal transformation*. Bantam.

Substance Abuse and Mental Health Services Administration. (2014). *A treatment improvement protocol: Trauma-informed care in behavioral health services*. TIP 57. US Department of Health and Human Services.

Walton, M. & Deming, W. E. (1988). *The Deming Management Method*. Perigee Books.

CHAPTER 2

The Impact of Urgency Culture on Self-Care

Jamie Doronkin

Introduction

As one of the opening chapters in this book about equity and organizational change for trauma-informed practices, this chapter provides foundational information to help unpack an important tenet:

The journey to equity begins with a deep dive into our internal beliefs about self-care.

This tenet is expanded upon in the last chapter of the book as part of a discussion about organizational improvement for trauma-informed practices. This chapter explores this beginning journey to equity by discussing self-care, the importance of needs, and the impact of urgency culture on the ability to care for the self in a way that honors needs and boundaries.

Self-Care as Learned from Others

Self-care has been most simply defined as "the set of activities in which one engages throughout life on a daily basis" (Sidani, 2003, p. 68). These activities include attempts to promote ideal health and prevent or manage illness (Woods, 1989) and can result in a range of experiences, depending on the activities and why they are being performed. As such, the implementation of self-care can be multi-faceted:

> Engaging in self-care is a process involving being aware of self, acquiring knowledge, and taking responsibility for meeting needs at whatever level they are presented. The performance of self-care behaviours can be influenced both positively and negatively by the attitudes of others. (Godfrey et al., 2010, p. 1351)

Self-care theory operates on the assumption that humans have the need to care for themselves (Easton, 1993). How individuals respond to this need, however, is influenced by factors such as self-concept, belief about competence and control over health, and perception of health status (Lachman, 1996; Sidani, 2003).

One of the most well-known theories on self-care, originally stemming from the nursing field, comes from Dorothea Orem's (2003) theory of self-care, which states that self-care behaviors are learned behaviors that purposively regulate human functioning and development and are composed of three conceptual elements:

1. Self-care—engaging in action to regulate functioning and development.

2. Self-care agency—operational powers or capabilities specific to performing actions of self-care.

3. Self-care requisites—requirements that guide the selection, choice, and conduct of regulatory actions in the care of self (Denyes et al., 2001).

The concept of *agent* is central to Orem's theory and refers to the ability to meet self-care requisites, such as gaining knowledge, making decisions, and taking action steps for change, all pieces that inform selection and choice (Steiger & Lipson, 1985).

Self-care, then, can be seen not only as a need (Easton, 1993) but as a birthright in which developing agency is crucial. Because the earliest models for self-care needs are caregivers, friends, family, co-workers, and classmates (Godfrey et al., 2010), self-care behavior patterns will likely match these first models witnessed. For example, if early models for self-care were centered on taking care of others first, even at personal sacrifice, then that is likely the self-care pattern that will be mirrored. Taking care of others first as a foundation for self-care can lead to a feeling of being trapped, as if there are no choices and that the needs of others must always come first. In this belief, one can eventually forget that personal needs exist at all (Bond, 2017).

Needs are the Seeds for Self-Care

This is how I lived for decades, as if I had no choices. I was unaware of my needs, and it began within my family culture. I grew up watching my mother always putting others before herself, many times to her detriment, and always from a stated belief that there was no other choice for her. As the oldest of five children, I was often praised as a teenager for putting myself last to help take care of my siblings in a home environment that was filled with traumatic events. It never occurred to me that I could put myself first or that my needs had a place in the household.

As a young adult, I chose to pursue a degree in special education because I wanted to make a difference for others. Having a career where I cared for others made sense to me, considering that so much of what I was taught and what I observed while growing up centered on self-sacrifice and caring for others. It was not until I sat in a therapist's office, well into my 40's—burned out from my life and my job—that self-care and the importance of having needs were discussed with me.

In this chapter, I share my understanding and growth around self-care, having needs, setting healthy boundaries, and the impact of current-day urgency culture on the innate human right to self-care. Through my perspectives as a teacher, researcher, university professor, and now self-care advocate, I share my journey in learning that *I actually have needs*, that they are important to honor, and that needs are the seeds for my self-care, especially the needs for physical well-being and connection (Bond, 2017; New York Center for Non-Violent Communication, 2015).

It is important here to talk about needs beyond just the basic physical well-being needs of air, food, water, and shelter. Needs are indeed the seeds for all self-care, including those more invisible beyond the obvious needs for physical well-being. While core needs for physical well-being are essential to our functioning and survival as humans, the following list brings attention to other important needs associated with values and the things humans desire, ranging from autonomy to play. These were the needs I had buried deep underneath my well-established role of caring for others, all at the expense of my well-being.

* Needs and Values: Things We All Want in Our Lives (Bond, 2017):

- Autonomy (which includes choice, dignity, self-expression)
- Connection (which includes acceptance, appreciation, belonging, security, self-care, self-expression)
- Meaning (which includes awareness, clarity, growth, perspective, self-expression)
- Peace (which includes balance, ease, order, space)
- Physical Well-Being (which includes air, food, water, sleep, self-care, safety)
- Play (which includes adventure, fun, joy, relaxation)

* For the full list of Needs and Values, go to the New York Center for Non-Violent Communication at: NBP Feelings and Needs Sheet—NYCNVC (https://www.nycvc.org/feelings-and-needs-sheet?rq=needs)

Urgency Culture: The Normalization of Ignoring Needs and Boundaries

In addition to some of the earliest influences on self-care needs, a newer phenomenon called *urgency culture* is fueling the normalization of ignoring needs and boundaries (Amir & Kahn, 2024). Urgency culture has gained momentum in recent years due to technological advancements influenced by social media (Kalman et al., 2021) and perpetuates a constant state of not being able to do enough fast enough to keep up with ever-increasing expectations (Thurrott, 2024). In this culture, there is not enough time to meet the constant demands of financial pressures, work obligations, family responsibilities, and taking care of ourselves and our needs (Estrada, 2024). Urgency culture is further fueled by globalized economic demands and the expectation of continuous productivity (Morales, 2023). The overriding theme in urgency culture is one of *never enough fast enough* while simultaneously trying to do everything (Estrada, 2024; Thurrott, 2024).

An Interruption of the Change Process

This culture has the potential to seemingly impact everything we do in our lives, with fast-paced expectations that do not allow for the process of change to unfold. For example, because urgency includes the expectation that people should be reachable at all times and respond to every query as if it is an emergency (Morales, 2023), the natural evolution of the change which involves assessing, considering needs, planning, and evaluation for adjustments never happens (Hiatt & Creasey, 2003). Additionally, because this culture is influenced by social media, which creates a sense of comparison and competition (Estrada, 2024), the typical vetting process of change plans can be compromised. Finally, because this culture is fueled by the notion that resources such as money and time are scarce (Fredberg & Pregmark, 2022), the willingness to consider multiple options cannot occur.

Shifting from Self-Care Demands to a Self-Care Journey

Research shows that individuals may abandon self-care when overwhelmed by symptoms or disability and/or when they feel that they are not supported (Godfrey et al., 2010). This was true for me in my self-care discovery journey. Initially, my self-care attempts were shrouded in an urgency culture, and I believed I had to make improvements quickly and successfully. As a chronic list maker, my original self-care list was a set of demands that added more pressure to do better, and to do it efficiently (see Table 2.1).

Table 2.1
My List of Demands

My Initial Self-Care Demands List
Find/make time for myself
Take better care of myself
Eat healthier
Do something from my bucket list
Get more sleep
Work fewer hours

Over time, as I learned about my needs, began to value them, and practiced setting boundaries, my self-care demands list evolved from a to-do list into an evolving inside journey.

Table 2.2
My Inside Journey

My Newer Evolution Toward Self-Care ... My Inside Journey
Learning about self-compassion
Learning about my wants and needs
Appreciating my wants and needs
Learning to ask for help when I need it
Learning how to say "*no*"
Learning how to hear/receive a "*no*"

An Assignment on Self-Care: "I Can't Take a Chance on Looking Needy."

Along the way, as I was working with teacher candidates, I discovered that one of the best ways to introduce needs and self-care was to require a self-care assignment. During a pre-student-teaching seminar, I would give students an assignment on self-care that required them to add two, five, ten, or 30 minutes of self-care into their day, each day, for four weeks. The times had to be pre-planned and reflected upon by seminar participants regarding their ability to meet the planned self-care activity and the need they believed it helped to meet.

The feedback from these teachers-in-training usually included these kinds of statements about the assignment:

- "I did this self-care project because it was an assignment and part of my grade. It was hard to do for four weeks, but I knew it would be over soon."
- "Honestly, I thought about cheating on the assignment, but I thought maybe there is something I can learn. Regardless, I can't take a chance on looking needy to my students."

Actually, though, that is a central key to self-care: recognizing and expressing our needs. It opposes the *culturally-shunned-looking-needy* by welcoming, discussing, and stating our needs with others, and is a beginning step toward breaking the cycle of sheltering needs and bypassing boundaries. This, however, is much easier said than done.

When Self-Care is Risky and Needs are Tucked Away for Safekeeping

As adults, if we have a trauma history, either as Adverse Childhood Experiences (ACEs) or Adverse Community Experiences, it may not be safe to show our needs or realize that we even have them (Smith et al., 2017; Venet, 2021). We may have been keeping them tucked away for safekeeping. We may not believe it is safe to show our needs—or even be in tune with them. None of this is a problem; it makes sense. If we grew up in a traumatic environment or household, as I did, then we can take solace in knowing that tucking away our needs is how we survived as children. As teachers and professionals working with students and others in the community who may also be growing up in traumatic environments, we can imagine that these individuals may also be tucking away their needs for safekeeping.

How can schools and other organizations begin to imagine a process for building a safe space for knowing and expressing needs, especially considering the increasing prevalence rates of ACEs on a national level (Crouch et al., 2019)? Several chapters in this book offer research and strategies in response to this question. This chapter invites a re-consideration of urgency culture in parallel with organizational improvement, specifically in relationship to John Kotter's eight steps for organizational change (1996/2012).

Urgency Culture vs. Creating a Sense of Urgency

In a well-established organizational improvement model developed by John Kotter (2008), urgency is used differently than in urgency culture. Creating *a sense of urgency* is often discussed as an initial step by Kotter and others to help foster momentum for change. In the context of initiating change actions for organizations, creating a sense of urgency can serve as a crucial catalyst for implementing improvements (Kotter, 2008; Oreg et al., 2011). While urgency culture is a growing and increasingly pervasive way of living, creating a sense of urgency for organizational improvement can fuel productivity and influence momentum for success, leading to true cultural changes (Kotter, 2008). See Table 2.3 for complementary parallels between urgency culture and creating a sense of urgency using Kotter's eight steps for change (1996/2012). These parallels will be revisited in the book's closing chapter as organizational change for trauma-informed practices is further considered.

Table 2.3
Complementary Parallels Between Urgency Culture and Kotter's Sense of Urgency

Urgency Culture Aspects as fueled by technological advancements, globalized economic demands (Estrada, 2024; Kalman et al., 2021; Morales, 2023; Thurrott, 2024).	**Creating a Sense of Urgency as the fueling first step of John Kotter's eight steps for organizational improvement** (Kotter, 1996/2008/2012).
A newer phenomenon influenced by social media.	1: A sense of urgency—influenced by an organization's most critical opportunities and hazards.
An expectation that people must be reachable at all times.	2: The guiding team—an expectation that change initiatives are ambitiously led by highly committed team members.
Responses to every question posed must be handled as if it is an emergency.	3: Visions and strategies—responses to challenges are guided by smart visions and strategies, even when the best strategies are elusive.
Resources, especially money and time, are scarce.	4: Communication—relentless communication of visions and strategies generates ongoing urgency as needed.
Comparison and competition abound as a constant standard.	5: Empowerment—to remove obstacles so visions can become reality.
An expectation that change must happen rapidly.	6: Short-term wins—guide empowerment and silence critics.
The theme of there is never enough fast enough abounds.	7: Never letting up—work builds on success and expands toward the realization of a vision.
The constant pressure of trying to do everything amid the expectation of continuous productivity.	8: Making change stick—changes become institutionalized into structures, systems, and culture.

Conclusion

For teachers and others in the helping professions who are experiencing the impact of urgency culture through mandated curricula, pedagogical changes, and mandated trainings (even those related to trauma-informed practices) without sustained support, the stage is set for ignoring personal needs and boundaries. This chapter intended to set a different stage, by discussing how self-care agency and personal agency are inextricably linked (Orem & Taylor, 2003) and shining a light on the importance of feeling in control over one's choices in life.

This chapter further intended to bring the power of personal agency to the forefront of equity and organizational change for trauma-informed practices, with this caveat: discovering one's own personal agency and power is a developmental process (Bindreiff, 2023) and evolves over time with support. While there are many avenues for personal empowerment, creating a sense of urgency to support this growth can be a central first step, while being mindful of the influences of urgency culture on our self-care agency.

References

Amir, Z., & Khan, A. Y. (2024). Relationship between social media addiction and urgency in young adults. *Journal of Professional & Applied Psychology*, *5*(3), 487–498.

Bond. T. (2017) *The Compassion Book: Lessons from the Compassion Course.* One Human Publishing.

Bindreiff, D. (2023, May 8). The trauma of adversity and the power of agency. https://corwin-connect.com/2023/05/the-trauma-of-adversity-and-the-power-of-agency/

Crouch, E., Probst, J. C., Radcliff, E., Bennett, K. J., & McKinney, S. H. (2019). Prevalence of adverse childhood experiences (ACEs) among US children. *Child abuse & neglect*, *92*, 209–218.

Denyes, M. J., Orem, D. E., & Bekel, G. (2001). Self-care: A foundational science. *Nursing science quarterly*, *14*(1), 48–54.

Easton, K. L. (1993). Defining the concept of self-care. *Rehabilitation Nursing*, *18*(6), 384–387.

Estrada, J. (2024, February 20). The therapist-approved way to protect your mental health from urgency culture. https://www.thezoereport.com/wellness/how-to-deal-with-urgency-culture

Fredberg, T., & Pregmark, J. E. (2022). Organizational transformation: Handling the double-edged sword of urgency. *Long Range Planning*, *55*(2), 1-19.

Godfrey, C. M., Harrison, M. B., Lysaght, R., Lamb, M., Graham, I. D., & Oakley, P. (2010). The experience of self-care: a systematic review. *JBI Evidence Synthesis*, *8*(34), 1351–1460.

Hiatt, J., & Creasey, T. (2003). Change management. *The people side of change.* Prosci.

Kalman, Y. M., Ballard, D. I., & Aguilar, A. M. (2021). Chronemic urgency in everyday digital communication. *Time & Society*, *30*(2), 153–175.

Kotter, J. P. (2008). *A sense of urgency*. Harvard Business Press.

Kotter, J. P. (1996). *Leading change*. Harvard Business School Press.

Kotter, J. P. (2012). *Leading change: With a new preface by the author*. Harvard Business School Press.

Lachman, V. D. (1996). Stress and self-care revisited: A literature review. *Holistic Nursing Practice*, *10*(2), 1–12.

Morales, M. (2023, January 24). Urgency culture: On the go or on the nerve? https://www.rtor.org/2023/01/24/urgency-culture-on-the-go-or-on-the-nerve/

Orem, D. E., & Taylor, S. G. (2003). *Self-care theory in nursing: Selected papers of Dorothea Orem*. Springer.

Oreg, S., Vakola, M., & Armenakis, A. (2011). Change recipients' reactions to organizational change: A 60-year review of quantitative studies. *The Journal of applied behavioral science*, *47*(4), 461–524.

Sidani S. (2003). Self-care. In D. M. Doran (Ed), *Nursing sensitive outcomes: State of the science* (pp. 65–113). Jones and Bartlett.

Smith, D., Frey N., Pumpian, I., & Fisher, D. (2017). *Building equity: Policies and practices to empower all learners*. ASCD.

Steiger, N. J., & Lipson, J. G. (1985). *Self-care nursing: Theory & practice*. Brady Communications.

Thurrott, S. (2024, July 7). Urgency culture: Feeling like you need to do everything right away. https://www.bannerhealth.com/healthcareblog/better-me/how-to-cope-with-urgency-culture-at-work-and-home

Venet, A. S. (2021). *Equity-centered trauma-informed education*. W. W. Norton and Company.

Woods, N. (1989). Conceptualizations of self-care: Toward health-oriented models. *Advances in Nursing Science*, *12*(1), 1–13.

CHAPTER 3

Undoing Urgency: Resisting Neoliberalism in Higher Education

CORINNE WOHLFORD MASON

THE COSTS OF HIGHER education have been especially contentious since the global economic crisis began in 2007. Today, in the context of the COVID-19 pandemic, the 2023–2024 Free Application for Federal Student Aid (FAFSA) crisis, and the so-called demographic cliff, to name just a few, post-secondary institutions have been under increasing pressure not just to cut costs but also prioritize "successful marketization and financialization as the driving purpose of higher education as a business" (Hall & Bowles, 2016, p. 30)—that is, to operate under the values of neoliberalism.

Neoliberalism as a *philosophy* dates to the post-World War II policies of economists like Friedrich Hayek, who opposed the New Deal government programs that Roosevelt had implemented to stimulate the economy during the Depression. In short, it prioritizes private market solutions over government interventions such as Roosevelt's. Neoliberalism took powerful hold in the United States and the United Kingdom in the 1980s as Ronald Reagan and Margaret Thatcher implemented reforms that reduced government spending on social programs while shifting rhetoric toward individual responsibility, self-help, and economic efficiencies. However, neoliberal *culture* is more than the sum of such policies. In this century, neoliberalism has become considered common sense and, as such, often goes unrecognized and unquestioned. It becomes internalized as the characteristics of a good person who must present as productive, healthy, and entrepreneurial; today, these are also the characteristics of a good student.

Neoliberal Culture and Higher Education

Under neoliberalism, post-secondary institutions' core missions move from creating knowledge to serving the public good toward economic efficiency, return on investment from more narrowly professionalized fields, and quantifiable measures of success. Corporate consultants hawk new models of a streamlined career-ready education with massive cuts to liberal arts programs and faculty. Political rhetoric that views education as elite, wasteful, or self-indulgent helps to justify these changes. Meanwhile, college students across the country struggle to meet basic needs, much less pay their tuition while proving themselves good students in this landscape.

Many commentaries on the intersection between neoliberalism and higher education have addressed how the corporatization of higher education affects labor—for instance, through overreliance on grossly underpaid contingent faculty and expectations for faculty and staff to do more with less. Others have focused on the increasing marginalization of the liberal arts, especially in the humanities, and have warned about the danger to democracy that disinvestment in fields such as art, history, philosophy, and literature represents. Without these fields, developing meaningful critiques of neoliberal culture becomes more difficult. Anil Balan (2023) writes, "Critics argue that the focus on economic efficiency and individual responsibility ignores the broader social and political contexts that influence economic outcomes and that neoliberal policies can exacerbate existing inequalities" (para 1).

As severe as these problems are for faculty and staff, the discourse around higher education and neoliberalism often overlooks the ways that neoliberalism affects students. These profound shifts have redefined what it means to become an educated citizen. Kathleen Lynch (2006) reflects on how universities operated in the past:

> Universities and other higher education institutions have marketed themselves in the public sphere and justified public funding for their activities on the grounds that they serve the public good. They have traded on their enlightenment inheritance that they are the guardians and creators of knowledge produced for the greater good of humanity. They are seen and claim to be seen as the watchdogs for the free interchange of ideas in a democratic society; they claim to work to protect freedom of thought, including the freedom to dis-

> sent from prevailing orthodoxies. They are quintessentially defined as public interest institutions and their research is granted status and credibility on the basis of its disinterestedness. (p. 1)

Today, by contrast, Hall and Bowles (2016) write:

> Both research and, critically, pedagogy are now governed by language rooted in productivity and organizational development. Externally, these priorities are expressed in truisms of strategic planning and university mission statements, so that 'real world solutions,' 'anytime, anywhere' technology, and 'career-ready graduates' are becoming familiar terms. Universities, like businesses, have refocused their strategic planning on market share and capitalization such that higher education is recruited to a national productivity agenda shaped around domestic and foreign investments and commodity productions. (p. 31)

Neoliberalism's ethos reshapes students into buyers and sellers, entrepreneurs who must be able to market themselves, compete with other students, and focus on what is often called the *return on investment* from their college majors so as not to be useless to society. It is understandable that students, especially those from working- and middle-class families who may be sacrificing greatly to fund their educations, prioritize social mobility. However, to access high-quality education, nearly all need to measure their success, or potential for success, in quantifiable measures such as grade point averages, standardized test scores, athletic statistics, and even the number and type of extracurricular activities—and leadership posts within extracurricular activities—that will earn them scholarships and, later (it is assumed), lucrative employment. This urgency culture and its constant demands to do more and be more mean that students' value is intrinsically linked to their productivity and quantifiable measures of success. Even volunteering in the community, which one might consider the quintessential service to the public good, becomes a line on a resumé that students can use to market themselves.

The Impact of Neoliberalism on Student Capacity to Learn

In this chapter, I explore the effects of neoliberalism on the student experience on campus, especially regarding mental health and the capacity to learn. Rather than focusing specifically on how neoliberal reform is remaking *what* is taught in universities, I argue that market-based values in education are hurting student learning because they have fundamentally altered students' self-worth and ideas about learning. Neoliberal values impede learning not only because they have fewer options for study but also because, by the time college students matriculate, they already have come to understand themselves as producers, achievers, and self-promoters who struggle to view education as exploratory or creative. The need to prove one's worth is especially intense for minoritized or low-income students, who have both social and financial incentives to prove they belong. Neoliberalism's profoundly ableist culture also devalues anyone with physical or mental barriers to measurable productivity.

Surviving University Life

I am a professor of the humanities. With an MFA in writing and a PhD in American studies, I have taught since 1999 a variety of courses in writing, literature, and US history and culture studies. Over the past quarter-century, I have taught humanities courses at five institutions, a mix of public and private, elite and non-elite, online and face-to-face, with and without religious affiliations, wealthy and struggling. Across the board, but especially as time has gone on, I, like many other educators, have encountered students who are terrified. They are exhausted, overwhelmed, and fearful. Increasingly, they struggle with anxiety, depression, and other forms of mental health challenges as they attempt to meet the financial, academic, and social demands of their lives. Neoliberalism's normalization of urgency and its emphasis on productivity and output define their self-expectations and college experiences.

My students are not alone. Mary Ellen Flannery (2023) writes in the National Education Association (NEA) News that in 2023, "The majority of college students (more than 60%) meet the criteria for at least one mental health problem—a nearly 50% increase since 2013. More than 80% report struggling at least somewhat" (The Depth of Mental Health Crisis section). Key challenges for these students are financial: they worry about how to pay for school and living expenses, how to find time to balance their work/studies/family obligations, and how to become employable after school. Anxiety and depression are common, and funding for counseling is often inadequate, in part because of cost savings by eliminating counseling services. Students report that in these contexts, it is simply more difficult to engage with their education: "They are also struggling with engagement and retention in the classroom; around six in ten (61%) say staying engaged and remaining interested in classes is a challenge" (Flannery, 2023, The Depth of Mental Health Crisis section).

Critics of neoliberalism suggest that, rather than conceiving of student wellness in terms of problems inherent in the student that require self-help, educators and administrators should look at the *political and social* contexts of these struggles. Hall and Bowles (2016) contend that the constant pressure on and resulting anxiety in college students are not "unintended consequence[s] or malfunction[s]" (p. 33) but rather natural consequences of learning under neoliberalism. Anxiety, they argue, "is inherent in the design of a system driven by imposing productivity and the potential for accumulation of capital" (p. 33). In a discussion of mental health and the neoliberal university, Michael Priestley (2018) is careful to note that there is no "universal causal relationship between neoliberal higher education policy and mentally ill health" (p. 186). Still, he suggests that educators should "identify the political, economic and social determinants of mental health" (p. 186), including the demands of neoliberal academic culture, in addition to providing therapy and counseling. Drawing on the work of philosopher Michel Foucault, Priestley conceives of the "existence, definition, explanation and treatment of mental 'illness' as an economic and moral construct that is both produced by, and reproduces, capitalism" (p. 186).

Priestley (2018) points to Foucault's notion of the self-policing subject, one who has internalized neoliberal value structures and so monitors oneself constantly by their benchmarks. He writes:

> Students subsequently revalue themselves and their productions according to their capital exchange value within neoliberal competition, which can lead to anxiety and perfectionism around certain assessment measures as well as intensification and lack of self-care and the internalisation of neoliberal competition and ranking structures. (p. 190)

Nadine Leese (2014) adds:

> The increasingly neoliberal organization of academic life creates and exacerbates experiences of mental illness and suffering, as well as making it difficult for people who are suffering to access support (or even just academia). The prevalence of mental illness in academia is not a wholly individual phenomenon, nor is it separable from the institutions in which individuals are embedded. As such, our responses to it need to go beyond how individuals might be 'included' or 'treated' or how they themselves might take responsibility for 'surviving' university life. (para 3)

Trauma and Trusting Relationships

Fallot and Harris (2009) define trauma in ways that align with what today's students are experiencing. They write that "trauma has often occurred in the service context itself" (p. 2). Here, they refer to social service agencies, but we might equally well apply them to schools—both secondary and post-secondary—as they prepare students to be marketable for admission and scholarships. Constant surveillance of one's grade point average, class rank, or standardized test scores—not to mention excelling in leadership positions in sports or student activities—stresses students, especially those with fewer resources. The authors underscore that "trauma is insidious and preys particularly on the more vulnerable among us" (p. 2), making it hard for people to form trusting relationships. Low-income students may be the most obviously affected, but neoliberal culture overlaps with racist, sexist, ableist, and homophobic culture such that one can understand how other marginalized students are at particular risk. But we might also do well to consider that the young are vulnerable, too. Many college students are on their own for the first time in their lives, struggling to meet their basic needs. Finally, Fallot and Harris (2009) explain that "trauma affects the way people approach potentially helpful relationships" (p. 2). This last point is especially relevant in the interaction between faculty and students; as students are traumatized by perceived expectations of perfection, they often perceive faculty members less as supportive mentors than as threats to their grade point averages. They are, in Fallot's and Harris' terms, "vigilant and suspicious" (p. 2).

This kind of trauma is harmful not only to student mental health but also to student learning. Learners are exhausted, overwhelmed, and fearful before they even matriculate. They distrust advisors and professors who may challenge their thinking or grade point averages. They neglect self-care. In her study of mental health and neoliberalism at Tufts University, Rachel Wahlert (2017) quotes one student: "Some people see health and happiness as more important than grades and college; I don't" (p. 86). They are tired from school, working to support themselves, trying to build a resumé for leadership positions and professionalizing experiences like internships. Neoliberalism's normalization of urgency defines their college experiences. One Yale University student related, "Everybody thinks that they're the only one who's suffering, so nobody says anything, so everybody suffers" (Wahlert, 2017, p. 87).

Strategies to Support Student Learning

In these contexts, students have fewer opportunities to take risks to use their imaginations in learning. They have less room to explore and diversify their fields of study. They avoid majoring in areas in which they have deep talents and abiding interests because they do not feel assured of a return on investment after graduation. They have learned to value instrumental skills over critical thinking. Traumatized learners struggle to let go of tried-and-true strategies. They want to know what will be on the test—how they will be measured—or cling to rubrics to satisfy minimum requirements. On research assignments, students often want to create an iron-clad thesis and outline before they have done any research to explore ideas, instead preferring only to find sources that confirm what they are saying. Too often, they turn to AI to think or write for them. I believe these are fear-based strategies that reflect the pressure to earn high marks and keep themselves financially safe and of economic value. In what follows, I relate some experiences in my own teaching and suggest some strategies for helping students resist this urgency.

An Assignment to Rest

Undoubtedly, my most useful undertaking to resist neoliberal culture was to teach a course on the topic itself. Arming students with this terminology, they easily identified how pervasive and even intimate these ideologies were in their own lives. After students read Tricia Hersey's (2022) *Rest is Resistance: A Manifesto*, I assigned students a rest requirement: they simply had to do something restful and unproductive over the course of a week, whether as daily practice or in one longer event. Nearly every student found some degree of difficulty in this project, feeling themselves wasting time, but that very difficulty, along with the deep discomfort about half felt with Hersey's book, also led to significant introspection and reflection on neoliberal culture in their lives.

In more everyday contexts, I avoid using PowerPoint or similar presentations in my teaching because students often transcribe them into their notebooks, seeing them as study guides rather than places for exploration or discussion. I hear from students that this approach was weird or unexpected but also that they preferred it; my course evaluations consistently demonstrate student engagement and interest. Whenever I can, I present assessments as open-ended. I often use short-essay quizzes of five or six questions, usually framed as *how does X contribute to* Y or *apply X author's idea to Y author's text*, so that the students are not simply regurgitating but having to think critically about intersections of ideas. I explicitly tell students that if they cannot show the relationships I'm seeking, they ought to write down whatever they know about X and Y so that I can award partial credit. However, when students write what they *do* know, they often start to make the hoped-for connections as they write, often to their surprise. Students often learn *while* taking their test and surprise themselves with their own learning.

A Two-Question Final Exam

The best final exam I ever gave was for a class that focused on the histories of race, gender, and social justice in the United States. Before the exam date, I told the students that there would be only two fill-in-the-blank questions: 1) Race and gender are _______; and 2) With regard to race and gender, social justice movements must ________. After giving them about 15 minutes to complete their sentences, I divided the students into small groups, each tasked with contributing one sentence for each question in an anonymous Google doc open to the class and projected on screen. No one received more credit or less for having been chosen. This step involved debate and negotiation: Which was the best answer? Why? What aspects had some answers left out?

Eavesdropping on the small group conversations and listening to the students earnestly debate what they had learned over the semester was a joy. They earnestly debated the merits of each statement. Laughter rang out at several moments, but their negotiations were substantive. After the groups anonymously added their sentences to the Google doc, with a different highlighter color for each group's response, we debated each as a class, ultimately choosing only one group's response for each question. Which was most inclusive, most representative, most clearly stated, most realistic? The students were competing, but only while laughing, knowing that no points were on the line for anyone. I was proud to see my students adeptly applying course concepts in their own words and with such apparent pleasure. After we chose the top sentence for each question, we then collectively edited the chosen sentences. How could we improve our chosen sentences? What should be added? Students were vocal and opinionated. Finally—and this was the only graded part of the assignment—the students wrote an individual response to this exercise: What do you see as the strengths and weaknesses of these summaries? What would you have added, subtracted, changed? Then, they annotated the sentences, pointing to at least three sources or concepts from our readings, class discussions, or other materials that would help support our sentences if they were to be remade into a longer essay form.

To put it plainly, my students loved this exam. The collaborative inquiry, the lack of pressure to memorize or even to plan beyond their personal first drafts of the summaries, and their increasing confidence as they *informally* fought for important course ideas reduced the stress of this assignment without sacrificing high-level thought and even accountability for texts and course concepts. The students seemed to enjoy rooting for their favorite anonymous sentences. It might seem as though this exercise reinforced the neoliberal value on competition, but in fact, the students seemed to *mock* this competitiveness, clearly playful, understanding that there were no stakes in having their own sentences chosen.

Clowning with ChatGPT

An exercise I called Clowning with ChatGPT was also helpful in dislodging neoliberal thinking. Almost universally, the students who turn to AI in unproductive ways are those who are most insecure or stressed, for one reason or another, and believe that AI will do a better job than they will. In a recent online composition course, however, I experimented with sending my students to ChatGPT at the beginning of the semester. The students asked the system to write them interpretive essays on various topics or events and then asked it to connect their topic to absurd other topics, such as *SpongeBob SquarePants*, and to share the results with commentary in the discussion board so that they could compare answers.

Students commented on the uniform ways ChatGPT responded, even when querying it about silly topics. They noticed the lack or the low quality of sources. They were dismayed at its inability to go beyond presentation of facts to making an actual argument. Working collectively, comparing their results with those of other students sharpened their distinctions between facts and critical thinking while laughing at some of the torturous connections the technology made between, say, SpongeBob and social determinants of health. Again, a sense of fun helped to unlock this lesson without the finger-wagging that often characterizes warnings about academic integrity. Students saw *why* I did not want them to use this tool for my course, such that I was not there to police them but to better coach them to a successful essay. That semester was the first since ChatGPT became prominent in which I detected no inappropriate use of AI in the course.

Design a Utopian Colony

In a social history course, students had been learning about the challenges of work, home, and family in the 1840s. In class, I gave them a brief overview of utopian colonies, popular in that decade, and then tasked them with using the rest of the period to design their own utopian colony that would solve the social problems we had studied. Students loved this project and often got very animated while they designed their colonies. I recall one memorable utopia in which the entire society functioned around butter: butter for sale, butter as worship, butter as food, butter as labor. Silly though it was, the students explained how they had reasoned through (while laughing a lot) the way their society addressed each social concern. Sharing our utopias was informal, even entertaining, but they demonstrated true engagement in a way that an exam question could not have elicited.

Laugh, Trust, Heal

None of these assignments or strategies is particularly innovative or revolutionary. But each of them was collaborative and fun without sacrificing critical thinking. Crucially, my ability to laugh with my students made me a more trustworthy instructor, even in online courses. My composition students complicated and deepened their writing, more willing to take chances in their writing. My history students increasingly moved away from the notion of history as a collection of facts to more critical interpretations.

And, also crucially, *I* laughed. I enjoyed my students in ways that kept my own and, thus, their morale up. Certainly, I have not fundamentally rid my students of neoliberal anxiety, but for small moments, collectively, we did lessen it. In this sense, I suggest that collegial *fun* is one way to build trust, give students a moment to breathe and think, and stress collective rather than individual success without pressure to measure, chart, and market ourselves (beyond selling a butter colony, that is!). Perhaps laughter, too, is resistance.

Drawing on bell hooks' (1994) *Teaching to Transgress: Education as the Practice of Freedom*, Hall and Bowles (2016) encourage educators to ask, "Where are the curriculum spaces inside formal higher education that enable the practice of freedom?" (p. 43). They challenge us to "consider how all instances of their curriculum... reproduce or refuse the ongoing colonisation of education by capital" as we attempt to "address the crisis of overwork and anxiety" (p. 43). To be sure, we must advocate for political reform and structural changes to support students in and outside the classroom. But where we can, we also might seek moments like the ones I have described, where students can laugh, rest, and collaborate as small acts of resistance, healing trauma through connection with themselves, their instructors, and one another, and surprising themselves as they discover what they did not realize they knew. These are not gamifications meant to stimulate more productivity. Rather, they empower *through* critical thinking, helping students discover the pleasure of inquiring into the world through different lenses. They are small moments of healing.

References

Balan, A. (2023). Neoliberalism, privatisation and marketisation: The implications for legal education in England and Wales. *Cogent Education*, *10*(2). https://doi.org/10.1080/2331186X.2023.2284548

Fallot, R. D., & Harris, M. (2009). Creating cultures of trauma-informed care. *Community Connections*. https://communityconnectionsdc.org

Flannery, M. E. (2023, March 29). *The Mental Health Crisis on College Campuses*. www.nea.org; National Education Association. https://www.nea.org/nea-today/all-news-articles/mental-health-crisis-college-campuses

Hall, R. & Bowles, K. (2016). Re-engineering higher education: The subsumption of academic labour and the exploitation of anxiety. *Workplace 28*, 30–47.

Hersey, T. (2022). *Rest is resistance: A manifesto*. Hachette UK.

hooks, b. (1994). *Teaching to Transgress: Education as the Practice of Freedom*. Routledge.

Leese, N. (2014, December 4). *Neoliberalism, mental health, and academia. Neoliberalism, Mental Health, & Academia – Dr Nadine Leese (nadinemuller.org)*

Lynch, K. (2006). Neo-liberalism and marketisation: The implications for higher education. *European Educational Research Journal*, *5*(1), 1–17.

Priestley, M. (2018). Sick of study: Student mental 'illness' and neoliberal higher education policy. In X. Shao, & E. Dobson (Eds.), *Imagining Better Education: Conference Proceedings 2018*, pp. 183–199.

Wahlert, R. (2017). Neoliberalism's war on undergraduate mental health. In Students of The Sociology of Higher Education, Fall 2017's *An Entrepreneurial University Revisited: The Continuing Transformation of Tufts, 2002–2017*, Tufts University. https://sites.tufts.edu/freedenblumeoeur/files/2012/08/Complete-book.pdf

CHAPTER 4

Understanding Elementary Student-Perceived Impact of Complex Trauma and Toxic Stress Response on Learning

JOANNE FISH

Introduction

A FEW YEARS AGO, I conducted a phenomenographic (Akerlind, 2005; Marton, 1986, 1988; Smith, 2005, 2006) research study in an urban fourth-grade classroom to discover how students (mostly nine- and ten-year-olds) who were exposed to traumatic events or complex trauma went about the work of learning. I wanted to know, from *their* perspectives, what it was like to attend to the daily cognitive demands of reading, writing, and other academic tasks, including being a community member of an inner-city classroom in an impoverished neighborhood.

To do this, I observed the students for about three hours a day, two days a week, for about five months. There were 19 students in the class. I received parental permission to interview a subset of eight of these students. With them, I conducted two interviews. In one I asked them questions from the Cameron Complex Trauma Interview (CCTI) (King et al., 2015) and also asked them to describe their home lives to me. In the second interview, I asked them questions from a Child and Youth Resilience Measure-12

(CYRM-12), a 12-question Likert scale measure of resilience factors (Liebenberg et al., 2013; Resilience Research Center, 2016) and asked them questions about events I had observed in the classroom.

This chapter is not a detailed academic accounting of the research as one might expect in a peer-reviewed article. Instead, I share some of the findings from classroom observations and student interviews. In this chapter, I also explore research around toxic stress response (Nelson et al., 2020) and the feasibility of using instruments such as the CYRM-12 (Liebenberg et al., 2013) to measure the impact of resilience and toxic stress on students' daily academic lives.

Location, Location, Location

This study took place in a small Catholic school situated just off a major highway in an inner-city, impoverished neighborhood. The student population was 100% African American. Students came to the school from a multitude of zip codes, and many came on scholarships. A historic parish church (built in the late 1800s) watched over the schoolhouse from across the street. It housed the cafeteria and gym. The school building, which was built in the late 1950s, was surrounded by abandoned buildings and rundown houses. My visits to the school were just a few years after the police-involved shooting death of Michael Brown. "Black Lives Matter" and "Hands Up—Don't Shoot" graffiti marked some of the abandoned buildings, a reminder of the racial inequities that contributed to the toxic stress and complex trauma students in the area experienced.

One day, while walking with her to the church across the street, the principal pointed out several bullet holes in the glass doors, allowing entry to the side of the church. She said there had been a gang shootout the night before. The neighborhood was generally quiet any time I was there, usually in the mornings during the week. Still, I was warned that the neighborhood evolved into a much more dangerous environment after dark. The bullet holes were a stark reminder of the community trauma that these students lived with daily.

When the principal gave me permission to do this study at the school, she suggested that I observe the fourth-grade classroom because she knew many of the students had some sort of trauma background. It soon became evident that this was certainly a good place to observe students who were attempting to learn, despite the tumultuous lives they lived outside of school hours.

Observations

I observed the class, usually in the mornings, from a corner in the back of the room, trying to be as unobtrusive as possible. Eventually, the students got used to me being there and all but ignored my presence (which is what ethnographic researchers strive for). Many days, the scene felt chaotic, with students milling around the classroom, some ignoring the teacher's requests to be seated. I got a sense that although she told me she had gone through trauma-informed training (she showed me a thick three-ring binder on top of a file cabinet) and that she practiced trauma-informed and (what she called) brain-based teaching, the teacher was in over her head. She often expressed frustration at this group of students and what she noted as their inability to focus on the tasks she had planned each day. During one of our talks she said, "This group is hard."

More than once, when students asked questions, she would retort with comments like, "I don't remember calling on you." "Remember when you raised your hand before? You should raise your hand when you ask a question." When one student asked (out of her own frustration), "Why don't you do what I asked?" The teacher replied, "Why don't you do what *I* asked?" I watched her jump from subject to subject with little organized transition time, and I had a hard time keeping up with what lesson the students were on, not to mention a lack of understanding of the learning objectives. I am unsure if I ever saw an entire lesson from start to finish because they would either run out of time or the teacher would stop it midway through because the students were not paying attention. While I wanted to focus my observations on the students, it was difficult not to take into account the teacher's actions and consider that those actions might be contributing to the students' complex trauma, creating even harsher toxic stress responses.

I saw this manifest in one young man, Zach (all names are pseudonyms), whose desk happened to be closest to me. More often than not, he spent class time doing everything but staying on task. I had noticed that he often struggled with reading and writing. He seemed to use negative behaviors to compensate for his lack of literacy skills. He was often out of his seat. He even crawled on the floor and out the door one day while the teacher was not paying attention. He eventually returned to the room, and I'm unsure whether she had noticed that he had been gone.

Zach's behaviors were not merely those of a student off-task, however. He often displayed bouts of anger towards either his teacher or peers. He easily became frustrated with schoolwork when he couldn't get help quickly enough. Anytime he was asked to write, he quickly gave up and would either completely disengage, laying his head down on his desk, or leave his seat to socialize with or antagonize his peers. I witnessed him slam his desktop down, angrily throw wadded-up paper and pencils, and even knock over a chair. He would sometimes attempt to read when asked to read silently, but I could tell that he often glossed over the text and feigned the act of reading. During one of our interviews, Zach revealed that reading was hard for him and that he had just started reading "big words."

When Zach answered the CCTI questions, he indicated that he had experienced several traumatic events. Among those events were that he had witnessed one cousin being arrested and that he heard gunshots in his neighborhood so often that he considered them to be "normal." Additionally, he had another cousin who had passed away, and he had seen his family members fight often. He said he "ignores it" when they do. For Zach, these occurrences may have been somewhat normalized in his life, but they no doubt contributed to complex trauma and what Nelson et al. (2020) call the *toxic stress response.* "Toxic stress is the maladaptive and chronically dysregulated stress response that occurs in relation to prolonged or severe early life adversity" (para. 5). Nelson et al. (2020) posit that the toxic stress response results in a disruption in brain development and other biological systems, potentially causing risk of both physical and mental disorders.

This is evident in the symptom check portion of the CCTI (Part Two). Zach indicated he had symptoms in several domains, including attachment (not feeling safe or not caring about others), biology (feeling ill or not wanting to be touched), affect regulation (getting upset easily, exploding, wanting to run away from situations, staying angry for a long time), behavioral (gets into trouble, needs routine), cognition (has problems staring or finishing tasks, difficulty paying attention), self-concept (negative self-image), and post-traumatic stress (watches out for danger, has scary dreams and/or flashbacks) (King et al., 2015). The areas in which there was more symptom intensity for Zach were biology, behavioral, and post-traumatic stress (King et al., 2015). These make sense when one considers my observations of Zach. He often ignored the teacher's commands and had somewhat explosive bouts of anger when he became frustrated. Interestingly, though, he scored a 30 out of 48 on the CYRM-12 (Liebenberg et al., 2013). This tells me that he *thinks* he is handling his stressors better than he is. It also makes sense that he says he often ignores them and attempts to normalize them. We will talk more about resilience and toxic stress response later in the chapter.

Two-thirds of children in the United States have experienced at least one traumatic event by the time they turn 16 (Centers for Disease Control, 2024). A 2023 poll, commissioned by Nemours©, KidsHealth© found that 37% of children report worrying at least once a week (Nemours Foundation, 2023). This chronic worrying can lead to anxiety, which, according to psychologists, leads to toxic stress (Nelson et al., 2020; Nemours Foundation, 2023). In a 2023 poll of more than 400 9–13-year-olds, Nemours Foundation discovered that 37% of children worry more often than once a week, while most children (86%) reported they worry at least sometimes. More troubling is that about a quarter of children (23%) feel as though no one notices when they feel worried (2023).

Constant worrying leads to stress, which causes children to be in a constant state of high alert. While it is normal for children to feel worried at times, prolonged worrying or anxiety leads to toxic stress response, which can interfere with schoolwork as well as their home and social lives (Shonkoff et al., 2021).

Teacher-Student Relationships Matter

Preliminary data analysis has indicated that the nature of interactions between the teacher and students is critical to student learning. Willis and Nagel (2015) have shown the vital role teachers play in elementary students' social, neurological, and psychological growth. Teachers should provide safety and security. Because teachers' roles in students' growth is highly significant (Alisic et al., 2012), they need to understand what students are thinking and feeling while attempting to do the work of learning and simultaneously navigating poverty, violence in the home, community trauma, and other stressors. I observed that when these students felt the teacher was attending to their needs, answering questions, and calling on them to help or read, they seemed to be more engaged than when they felt ignored or not heard. Accordingly, interview responses of several students included comments about feelings of frustration when the classroom teacher seemingly ignored their questions or needs.

Given that interviews occurred at the end of the observation period and afterwards, students were asked to reflect on specific incidents and explain their thoughts and feelings. A specific example of this is when one female, Rilee, was asked about an incident in class when she became visibly angry and refused to work. When asked why she acted that way, Rilee replied, "Because she makes me mad! She doesn't ever answer my questions." Rilee's reactions to the teacher's seemingly adversarial responses to Rilee's needs mimic what King et al., (2013) referred to as complex trauma symptoms and what Nelson (2020) might categorize as a toxic stress response. These included often being off-task and sometimes verbally aggressive. Rilee was frequently out of her seat and talking with other students. When redirected by the teacher, Rilee would seemingly ignore the request or simply refuse to comply. Refusal would often be met with a raised voice and talking back to the teacher.

Not surprisingly, during the CCTI interview, Rilee's responses indicated the presence of trauma. In her young life, an uncle had died at an early age, and she said that she often heard gunshots outside her home. Additionally, her dad lived out of town, and she did not get to see him very often. Did these adverse experiences impact Rilee's learning and ability to consistently comply with classroom rules? She seemed to have a hard time waiting to be called on when she had her hand up for questions, and when she had to wait more than a few seconds, she would go off-task, talk with other students, and sometimes get into arguments with peers and her teacher.

When noting the symptom intensity that Rilee's interview revealed, her lack of ability to stay on task makes sense because this resides in the cognitive domain (King et al., 2015), which was an intensity area for her. Other areas of symptom intensity were biology (she sometimes complained of a headache), affect regulation (she would find ways to avoid academic work and get upset easily and stay that way), and post-traumatic stress (she said she sometimes had scary dreams and was always looking out for danger). She scored 32 out of 48 on the resilience scale (Liebenberg et al., 2013), which is interesting and is discussed further in the next section.

Is Perceived Resilience the Reality?

According to the National Child Traumatic Stress Network (NCTS), resilience is "the ability of a child to recover and show early and effective adaptation following a potentially traumatic event" (n.d., p. 1). Interestingly, seven of the eight students I interviewed scored 30 or above (out of a possible 48) on the CYRM-12 (Liebenberg et al., 2013). The one student who didn't scored a respectable 29. So, would these results indicate that these students might be able to overcome trauma events and toxic stress in their lives and still perform well academically in spite of those adverse events? Perhaps a better question is, what does it say about *their perspectives* of the complex trauma they experience?

Russell et al. (2021) caution researchers not to put too much stake into data gleaned from measures taken at a single point in time, which is the case for this study. They note, "Individual factors that promote resilience as it relates to particular outcomes will depend on the individual and the context of the risk, with different types of adversity calling for various skill sets and protective factors that may vary across settings" (para. 3). The very nature of youth and adolescent development, along with how various factors in their lives may evolve over time, make it difficult to document factors promoting resilience and its impact during any one study. Rather, they argue for longitudinal studies that collect data over time. This dynamic process should be based on interactions that are both "inter- and intrapersonal, as well as contextual" (Russell et al., 2021, para. 3).

In the case of this study's fourth-grade participants, a number of factors needed to be considered. For example, Zach had noted that he ignored his family members' fighting and that, while it was sad when his cousin died, he chose not to think about it. He also attempted to normalize hearing gunshots outside his home. These all seemed to be ways for him to compensate for the toxic stress responses that he seemed to be displaying in his anger during school. Because the CYRM-12 was used as a self-reported measure in this study, the results might have been a bit skewed. The answers were Zach's *perception* of the protective factors in his daily life. I would argue, however, that, based on Zach's actions, he was experiencing a toxic stress response (Nelson et al., 2020), and this was manifested at school.

Zach's response to the complex trauma he lived with, his misbehavior and frustrations at school, seemed to be contributed to a classic toxic stress response as described by Franke (2014). Franke (2014) notes that the toxic stress response affects the "neuroendocrine-immune network, and the response leads to a prolonged and abnormal cortisol response" (para. 8). This results in a dysregulated immune system, leading to a persistent inflammatory state that increases the risk of illnesses in children and adults (Fagundes et al., 2013). Additionally, the toxic stress response can play a role in mental health ailments such as depressive disorders, behavioral dysregulations, PTSD, and psychosis as it negatively impacts the limbic system (Murphy et al., 2022). All this fits with how Zach acted in the classroom.

Conclusion

Attempting to uncover and report on children's perspectives of how their own trauma impacts their work of learning is not only a daunting task but a tricky one. It is a complex endeavor that demands diligence and that researchers keep an open mindset. Gathering the data was complicated. I wanted to be embedded in the class, but other obligations created limitations on the amount of time I could spend observing.

I wanted to gather valid and reliable data beyond my observation notes, which is why I used the CCTI and the CYRM-12. These proved to be valuable because, along with a review of the literature, they offered structured insight into what I was observing and helped me put my observations into perspective.

One set of data that I was unable to gather was interview data from parents and caregivers. This was part of the study plan, and there were parents of the eight students I interviewed who had agreed to talk with me, but connecting with them proved to be impossible. I finally abandoned that idea, lamenting the loss of valuable data to create a rich context for the student-participant data.

Given the need for additional research, I would encourage other researchers to design longitudinal studies that follow a cohort of students into adulthood, as suggested by Franke (2014). They could conduct multiple interviews and get a variety of insights as participants mature. They could also collect data on participants' academic records, employment records, significant life events, and health information. We have scientific data that shows the impact of trauma and toxic stress on our brains and our bodies, but until we can learn more about how our younger student population thinks about it, we are only guessing when it comes to determining how best to meet their needs.

References

Akerlind, G. (2005). Learning about phenomenography: Interviewing, data analysis and the qualitative research paradigm. In J. Bowden, & P. Green (Eds.), *Doing Developmental Phenomenography* (pp. 63–73). RMIT Press.

Alisic, E., Bus, M., Dulack, W., Pennings, L., & Splinter, J. (2012). Teachers' experiences supporting children after traumatic exposure. *Journal of Traumatic Stress, 25*, 98–101.

Centers for Disease Control. (2024, October 8). About Adverse Childhood Experiences. Adverse Childhood Experiences (ACEs). https://www.cdc.gov/aces/about/index.html

Fagundes, C. P., Glaser, R., & Kiecolt-Glaser, J. K. (2013). Stressful early life experiences and immune dysregulation across the lifespan. *Brain, Behavior, and Immunity*, *27*, 8–12.

Franke H. A. (2014). Toxic stress: Effects, prevention and treatment. *Children (Basel, Switzerland)*, *1*(3), 390–402. https://doi.org/10.3390/children1030390

King, J., Solomon, P., Ford, J. (2015). The Cameron Complex Trauma Interview.

King, J., Solomon, P., & Ford, J. (2017). The Cameron Complex Trauma Interview (CCTI): Development, psychometric properties, and clinical utility. *Psychol Trauma*, *9*(1), 18–22. https://doi.org/10.1037/tra0000138

Liebenberg, L., Ungar, M., & LeBlanc, J. C. (2013). The CYRM-12: A brief measure of resilience. *Canadian Journal of Public Health = Revue canadienne de sante publique*, *104*(2), e131–e135. https://doi.org/10.1007/BF03405676

Marton, F. (1986). Phenomenography: A research approach to investigating different understandings of reality. *Journal of Thought, 21*(3), 28-49.

Marton, F. (1988). Phenomenography: Exploring different conceptions of reality. In D. Fetterman (Ed.), *Qualitative approaches to evaluation in education: The silent scientific revolution* (pp. 176–205). Praeger.

Murphy, F., Nasa, A., Cullinane, D., Raajakesary, K., Gazzaz, A., Sooknarine, V., Haines, M., Roman, E., Kelly, L., O'Neill, A., Cannon, M., & Roddy, D. W. (2022). Childhood trauma, the HPA axis and psychiatric illnesses: A targeted literature synthesis. *Frontiers in Psychiatry*, *13*, Article 748372. https://doi.org/10.3389/fpsyt.2022.748372

National Child Traumatic Stress Network. (n.d.). *Resilience and Child Traumatic Stress*. https://www.nctsn.org/sites/dfault/files/resources/resilience_and_child_traumatic_stress.pdf

Nelson, C. A., Bhutta, Z. A., Harris, N. B., Danese, A., & Samara, M. (2020). Adversity in childhood is linked to mental and physical health throughout life. *The BMJ*, 371, m3048. https://doi.org/10.1136/bmj.m3048

Nemours Foundation. (2023). What's worrying America's kids – A national survey by Nemours©, KidsHealth©. Nemours Foundation.

Resilience Research Centre. (2016). Child and youth resilience measure.

Russell, B. S., Collins, C. M., Tomkunas, A. J., & Hutchison, M. (2021). Exploring the factor structure of the child and youth resilience measure (CYRM-12) for young children in a disadvantaged community. *Children and Youth Services Review*, *120*, Article 105746. https://doi.org/10.1016/j.childyouth.2020.105746.

Shonkoff, J. P., Slopen, N., & Williams, D. R. (2021). Early childhood adversity, toxic stress, and the impacts of racism on the foundations of health. *Annual Review of Public Health*, *42*(1), 115-134.

Smith, D. E. (2005). *Institutional ethnography: A sociology for people.* AltaMira Press.

Smith, D. E. (2006). *Institutional ethnography as practice.* Rowman & Littlefield Publishers, Inc.

Sorich, E. (2023, February 28). Most Americans experience a traumatic event by the age of 16 - Here are the symptoms. Charlie Health. https://www.charliehealth.com/research/most-americans-experience-a-traumatic-event-by-the-age-of-16-here-are-common-symptoms

Willis, A., & Nagel, M. (2015). The role that teachers play in overcoming the effects of stress and trauma on children's social psychological development: Evidence from Northern Uganda. *Social Psychology of Education, 18*(37), 37–54.

CHAPTER 5

Designing a Classroom Space for Middle School Students to Experience Empowerment Through Choices

Haley Porter

Introduction

Imagine that the last time you saw your mother was when you left the house while she was lying in bed, only to return after school to find she had died in her sleep, or seeing your mother shot point blank by her boyfriend while holding your younger sibling in her lap. How do you stay awake in class when you are so tired from being awake all night because the sounds of gunshots and sirens keep you from sleeping, or when you are feeling that ache and emptiness in your stomach that makes it hard to focus because the last time you ate was at school during lunch the previous day? While these events may seem like rare occurrences, the sad truth is that they are not; they are part of a trend of increasing adverse childhood experiences across our nation. Data from the 2016 and 2020 National Survey of Children's Health (NSCH) show significant year-over-year increases in diagnosed behavioral or conduct problems in children, increases in unmet healthcare needs, and increases in the number of children whose parents struggle with job stability and childcare resources (Lebrun-Harris et al., 2022). Additional research indicates that just under half (45%) of children in the United States have experienced at least one adverse childhood experience, with about one in ten children having experienced three or more adverse childhood experiences (Crouch et al., 2019). Economic hardship and divorce or separation of parents or guardians are the most common adversities reported in all states nationwide (Sacks & Murphey, 2018).

The impacts of these experiences are present in schools across the nation, including the middle school where I teach, which is located in a significantly under-resourced urban public school district. My adolescent students carry the impact of these and other adverse experiences with them, sometimes silently and sometimes not so silently, into their classes with me. This chapter shares what I have learned from these students over the years and how that has guided me in creating a safe space in which they find empowerment through the belief that they have choices.

When Middle School Students Carry Trauma to School

The experiences from adult-driven traumatic events often result in middle schoolers feeling as if they need to present themselves as being much more mature than they are. However, it is important to remember they are still children—adolescents between childhood and adulthood, struggling to figure out their emotions, responsibilities, relationships with peers and family members, and themselves. Students who then have trauma added to an already complicated time in their lives have even more to try to process. How they process this trauma can significantly affect their behavior, performance, and relationships in and out of the classroom (Murphey & Sacks, 2019).

Providing a safe environment for all students, especially those who carry these burdens, is just as important as providing an education (Darling-Hammond & DePaoli, 2020; Chafouleas et al., 2016). Creating a safe environment is imperative when teaching students who are faced with trauma that no young person should ever have to endure. A safe environment is not just physical; emotional space is equally important. The classroom environment should not only provide safety for students but also allow for support to talk about and process the trauma if desired. Students need not feel judged or be faced with triggers that make the trauma worse. They need to know that the adults at school can be trusted, so they have people to help them navigate this new and confusing time. These supporting adults can help middle school students who are struggling to adapt to their growing bodies, new emotions, and more complex relationships, and help them better cope with the trauma they have in their lives.

A Space That Belongs to the Students

"Wow! This feels like a home!" These six words drive me to create a physical space where students, especially those who come to school with the weight of the world on their shoulders, can feel safe. From the first day of school, creating relationships with students is a critical part of education and begins with positive first impressions. Relationship building is where the opportunity to create an emotionally safe environment begins. At the school where I teach, most of our students are affected by trauma. I have taught students who are homeless, students who have been subjected to abuse of all forms, students whose parents are incarcerated, students who have witnessed assaults including murders, and students faced with food and basic needs insecurities. These are just the beginning of the traumas experienced by our middle school students. To be effective in the classroom, it is essential to recognize and understand the trauma students experience outside the classroom.

These students are seeking a safe place where they can relax, if only for the hours they are in school. Their classroom becomes their home for those hours, and how they are spent can make a difference in the relationships they form. I spent hours during the summer thinking of ways to make a classroom with limited flexibility a place where students feel safe, and it was worth every minute of the personal time sacrificed. In the fall, I added lamps to soften the mood, so the harsh overhead ceiling lights could be turned off. For those times that more light is needed, I added light covers over the fluorescent lights to lessen the harshness.

I use music to match the mood of the class during different lessons. I play soft, relaxing music while students work independently and play music of their taste when they need a little motivation to keep working. I added a reading nook/quiet corner that allows students to have a place in the classroom to take a break. The quiet corner has a comfy couch and chair with a soft, shaggy rug surrounded by LED lights. It is tucked in the back of the classroom to serve a dual purpose. First, it is a reward when a student has completed all their work and wants a few minutes to decompress, listen to music, read, or relax. The second purpose is to allow students who need a mental break, whether during my class or if they are struggling in another class, to use our room as their buddy room. It allows them to cool off if needed before they get involved in a confrontation with another teacher or student. It also allows them to nap on a day when they did not get much sleep the night before. I even added a water cooler because our water fountains in the school are often not working, leaving students with few options for fresh water throughout the day.

Creating an Emotionally Safe Space

To create an emotionally safe space, students must feel they are heard (US Department of Education, 2021) and can express themselves and share things about themselves without judgment or criticism. At the beginning of each year, I stress the importance of respect towards one another, respect towards me, and my respect towards them. I explain how everyone in our classroom deserves the same opportunity to express their thoughts and opinions without judgment. Moreover, perhaps most importantly, I explain that what is shared in our classroom, whether expressed aloud or shared in their writings, does not leave the classroom. I do not tell other teachers, administrators, or staff what students share if their safety and security are not at risk.

Building Trust

Once students begin to trust their teachers, they may begin to share very personal information with them, and teachers need to be prepared to handle the shared information and be flexible to sometimes bend the rules. I will use cell phones as an example. Students must turn in their cell phones each day before school begins. This is a school-wide policy used to limit the distractions cell phones can cause. Not a school year has gone by when I have not had at least one student with an incarcerated parent. There have been instances when those students will come to me and explain that they did not turn their cell phone in on a particular day because their parent was going to call them from prison. I have bent the rules on those days and allowed them to step out of the classroom when the call comes in because I believe it is more important to allow a child to have contact with a parent who has limited opportunities to communicate than to stick to a particular rule, especially when that student trusted me enough to share that information.

Providing Student Collaboration and Choice

Reflection on the previous year also plays into ways to improve the classroom and make it one where students can feel safe. I ask for student feedback through an end-of-the-year survey and document conversations with students throughout the school year. I note what students tell me made them feel more successful, what made them feel safe, or what helped them on a difficult day. One student left me this message:

> *Hello Mrs. Porter,*
>
> *I wanted you to know that I appreciate you and everything that you do for your classes. ...Your class has been the one class in which we can express ourselves and our opinions. You also may not remember, but while I was struggling with home issues and began to fall behind in school, you were one of the few teachers I felt I could confide in. I'm honestly grateful to have you and your class this year.*

This feedback helps me understand what is important to my students and aids me in prioritizing my instructional choices. For example, students have expressed the need for more collaborative projects, more time allowed to turn in work, allowing them to eat snacks during class, and allowing them to choose their seats. Another student expressed their appreciation in rhyme:

> *Ms. Porter, dear teacher of mine,*
>
> *Your lessons are like rays of sunshine brightening my path and lighting my way, guiding me through each and every day.*
>
> *With patience and guidance, you teach us all, never letting anyone feel small. You push us to do our very best and help us overcome any test. You instill in us a love of learning and inspire us to keep*

yearning to reach for the stars and follow our dreams no matter how hard it seems.

Other feedback, such as allowing students to choose their seats, is one suggestion I work into the school year gradually. Students have told me they appreciate the opportunity to express their opinions and not be judged. They appreciated extra time or alternative ways to turn in homework when their access to technology was limited, especially at home. They have also told me how they appreciated that I was a teacher who kept her word, whether that meant in the rewards offered or a punishment when the class did not adhere to class rules. Students will also provide feedback of a more personal nature. For example, one student told me how much he appreciated the Lunchables I kept in my mini fridge for all the days he did not have anything for lunch. Another student appreciated the breakfast items I kept in my room for the days he did not have time to eat before coming to school.

Building Trust Through Relationships

Perhaps the most feedback I receive year after year from students is how they appreciate having someone listen to them and allow them to tell a teacher what they need to be successful.

Students who have experienced trauma frequently have trust issues. They have had adults in their lives whom they trusted; then, they were let down. They have other teachers who have discounted them and told them they will not amount to anything or will be unsuccessful. Some students have experienced trauma through abuse from someone they should have been able to trust.

Building trust takes time and effort. Students will not simply enter a classroom on the first day of school and trust the teacher standing before them. A teacher must prove to a student that they can be trusted. Building trust between the teacher and students is essential during the first two weeks of each school year when relationships begin to form and is a powerful tool for students' learning (Smith et al., 2017). Even after those first two weeks, with numerous relationship-building exercises and assignments, the presence of trust and security is not a given. Building trust is an ongoing process that continues throughout the school year.

Back-to-School Survey

One activity I believe is of utmost importance is the back-to-school survey I give students. The survey asks students a variety of questions that not only allow them to share fun facts about themselves but also provide meaningful insight into what the students face in their personal lives. I ask the general *get-to-know-you* questions that serve as icebreakers, but the other questions provide much more insightful information. Examples of these include who they live with, the best way to reach the person they would like me to contact to share important information, the number of siblings they have (I make sure to clarify siblings on *both sides* of the family), and one thing they believe I should know about them that will make them successful in class.

I keep these surveys in a folder and refer to them throughout the school year. I also use this information throughout the year when using examples during lessons or writing prompts during journaling. I try to avoid making generalized statements about topics that may not apply to all students. For example, I do not ask where students went during summer or spring break, what students received for their birthday or Christmas, or topics about mothers and fathers. Many of my students do not live with one or both parents, and many do not have the financial means to take vacations or receive gifts for birthdays or Christmas. The information I gather from these surveys can help avoid triggering students who experience trauma in their home lives. Additionally, I update the contact information as needed because parents or guardians often change addresses, phone numbers, and email addresses. I make notes on these surveys throughout the year as I learn new things about my students. Knowing things such as what sports they play, their birthday, important dates, and if I taught a sibling in previous years is an important and effective way to build a strong relationship with a student.

Enhancing Student Choice and Voice

For students to take ownership of their classroom and, ultimately, their actions, they need to understand that they have choices in the classroom (Brooks & Young, 2011). Student choice can provide a sense of security for students whose lives outside the classroom leave them with little choice and almost no voice (Walter et al., 2008). When students are provided choices within the safety of the classroom, seeds for empowerment are planted, and those seeds should be planted early in the school year (Platt, 2018).

Classroom Rules

At the beginning of each year, it is part of the procedure for teachers to explain the classroom rules and expectations. Often, teachers provide students with a list of those rules and expectations. One alternative to this process, which allows students to have more of a voice in their classroom, is to allow students to develop the rules and expectations. Let's face it, no one likes to hear what they can and cannot do in a space where they will be spending much of their time, and this is especially true for middle schoolers. Students know what works for them and what is just not that important. Even those students who become disruptive understand what they should and should not be doing. When a teacher allows students to take responsibility for creating rules and expectations for their classroom, and the students express their expectations of themselves and their classmates, this becomes the first step in their taking ownership of their classroom.

Sticky Notes Activity

During the first week of school, each class decides what rules they would like to implement in their classroom. I give each student two sticky notes and ask them to write two rules they think will make it possible for them to be successful in class. I present a list of the rules previous classes have decided on as a guide and limit class rules to five, so students need to focus on what is most important. Once students write down their rules, they post the notes on an anchor chart. I gather the sticky notes and tally the results. The top five rules become the rules for the class. I then type up those rules and add them to an Our Class Rules bulletin board along with the consequences of violating the rules. Students are made aware of these consequences before they write down their rules so that they know what to expect if the rules are broken.

The consequences are standard consequences that the eighth-grade teacher team has determined along with the administration. The consequences for breaking a class rule include: (1) the first violation is a five-minute meeting during lunch to discuss the inappropriate behavior; (2) the second violation is a meeting during lunch to call parents and discuss the inappropriate behavior; (3) the third violation is a meeting with the teacher during lunch, a referral to the Positive Behavioral Interventions and Supports (PBIS) and social support team, and a write-up; (4) the fourth violation is a behavior referral to administration, request for an in-person meeting with parents, and a behavioral write-up.

Teachers may be surprised by how closely the students' list of rules and expectations resembles ones they would have created without student voices. This is especially true for students whose lives are often chaotic and trauma filled. One thing they crave, especially at school, is a calm, organized, respectful space where their voices can be heard and where they feel safe expressing themselves.

What Appears to be a Choice Can be Trauma in Disguise

Permitting students to make choices is something that continues after those first few weeks of school. Sometimes, what appears to be a choice, such as not turning in homework or assignments, can often be out of a student's control. There can often be factors that prevent students from completing work, including having the responsibility of watching younger siblings once they get home from school, not having wi-fi or electricity at home, or even homelessness. It is also essential to understand that students who experience trauma may simply not be able to focus on homework once they leave the school building. This is not their choice; it is the life in which they live. Finding alternative ways for students to complete their work is essential, and it requires flexibility and understanding. This can not only improve student achievement but also provide those students with another choice and the opportunity to be seen.

In a world where most schoolwork relies on the ability to use and access technology, it can be challenging to adjust assignments and homework for students who need help to complete the work. However, students who lack access to technology outside the classroom are placed in another stressful situation over which they have little or no control. Being mindful of this and having alternative ways for students to complete work are essential. Teachers should print off those digital assignments and allow students to respond orally to questions. Finding alternative times at school for students to complete their work can give those students back the choice to complete their work and be successful in school.

The decision to allow flexibility in submitting work has made a world of difference in some relationships I formed with students, and one particular student comes to mind who demonstrates how important this can be. During the first part of the school year, she and I butted heads on just about everything. She came to class late nearly every day, rarely turned in assignments, and challenged me at every chance she could. After losing or damaging two iPads, she no longer had access to technology. Once I learned this and learned of her home life, which caused much of the combative attitude she came to school with each day, I knew the only way for her to be successful was to give her some of the control over issues we were butting heads about each day.

She came into class one day, and I handed her a folder of all the missing assignments she had that were previously all digital. She looked at me and asked if I would allow her to complete them and take her textbook home (which I do not usually allow). I said yes, even to the assignments that were beyond the time I would accept late work and asked that she submit everything within the next week. Two days later, she had completed all the assignments, and they were all done well. I made sure to grade her work immediately that day after school and updated her grade in the grading system. She went from a failing grade to a passing grade in two days. The day after she saw her grade, she came into class, gave me a hug, and took her seat. No words needed to be shared; the hug said it all. For the rest of the year, she continued to keep up with her work and would let me know if anything was happening that was preventing her from completing her work. She became her own advocate and took responsibility for her successes, but she also knew I was there to help her every step of the way.

Once students take ownership of their work and their classroom, watching how protective they become over their space is fascinating. Students begin to enforce the classroom rules with little teacher input. Students voluntarily clean up the classroom, monitor explicit language, make others who are not in their class aware of the classroom rules and expectations, and take pride in the classroom they have created. Students will correct other students' behavior. They explain that certain words are not allowed in our classroom and that before they take something, such as a cup of water from the water cooler, they need to ask for permission. They even clean up the classroom on days when I have been out and a substitute has been in the room. They understand that the way the classroom looks is a reflection on them—it is their space, and they make sure it is respected.

Collaborative Learning

During my first two years of teaching, I struggled with classroom management, student engagement, and student participation. After much reflection and an excellent mentor teacher, I recognized these struggles partly stemmed from my inflexibility. I knew changes needed to be made, but figuring out where to begin took a lot of work. Knowing I had nothing to lose, I decided to ask students what worked and did not work for them. I wanted to have their input. When I started listening more to student feedback, I realized how much easier classroom management, student engagement, and student achievement could become.

I realize the risk I take when asking students for this type of feedback. Students have become accustomed to voicing their opinions at my end-of-the-year survey or roundtable and do not hold back. Several times, I have been caught off guard by the honesty of middle school students. Being a middle school teacher requires a thick skin and the ability to laugh, even when it is at your own expense.

One of the biggest lessons learned was to allow students to work together more often. I realized how vital collaboration is, not only for students who are struggling academically but also for those struggling with emotional or personal issues that prevent them from completing work alone or outside of class hours. Allowing students to collaborate on assignments and projects encourages participation and improves work quality. Collaboration is also a crucial life skill that, when learned early, can benefit them throughout their academic career and beyond (Smith et al., 2017). Once I released some of this control to the students and allowed them to make some of their own academic decisions, the most significant improvements I observed were participation in daily assignments and building a stronger sense of community within the classroom. Students began listening and learning from one another. This, again, is another crucial life skill that needs to be introduced early in academic life. Students learn how to work through disagreements respectfully and learn to listen to the voices of others.

Student Empowerment Through Trauma-Informed Practices and Writing

Writing is essential in building trust while satisfying the curriculum requirements in a language arts classroom. In the eighth grade, students must learn formal and informal writing and how to switch between the two. The first informal writing assignment is a journal assignment, which serves a dual purpose. It allows me to evaluate students' writing and is another opportunity to earn their trust.

Composition notebooks are provided for each student. This is intentional because by having the same notebook for all students, students will not know whose notebook it is because they all look the same on the outside when they choose to share their journals. A twenty-minute timer is set, and students are told to write whatever comes into their minds until the timer sounds. There will always be a student who needs help figuring out what to write. Having writing prompts available can help a student get started in the journaling process. Topics may include: Tell me about a time when you were successful when you thought you might not have been. If you could travel anywhere in the world, where would it be? Tell me about a time when you stood up for someone or someone stood up for you. I try to keep the first writing prompt as positive as possible.

I use information from the back-to-school surveys to create other writing prompts that are applicable to that year's class. I avoid choosing topics that can be triggering for students, such as what they did over the summer, a story about their family, their favorite birthday, or their best vacation. These topics can be difficult for a student who may have experienced something traumatic or may not have the financial means to celebrate birthdays or holidays. For students who experience economic issues, summer and long extended breaks are often not the best time due to food insecurity or lack of other necessities provided during the school year. Being mindful of these situations can allow a student to participate in writing without feeling ashamed.

Once students have journaled for a set amount of time, they can decide if they want me to read their journals. There are two identical boxes for each class. One box at the front of the class is the *To Read* box, and one at the back of the room is the *Not to Read* box. Each time they journal, students decide if they want me to read their journals. They know that if they choose for me to read an entry, the journal will never leave the room, and the information they share will never be discussed with another person unless it is a matter of their safety.

The first journal assignment of the year is eye-opening and a learning experience. One or two students will test me each year during this first assignment. They will ask if they can cuss in their journal, to which the answer for this assignment would be no, with the explanation of keeping things respectful. Students have also asked if they can draw something instead of writing. I do allow this sometimes but explain there will be times when this will not be an option. When students decide to let me read their journals, I always respond in writing with a short response or answer a question they may have asked in the journal. Students want to know that we are interested in what they have to say and that we will take the time to read their writing.

Standards-Based Formal Writing Requirements

Formal writing can also be mutually beneficial. Essays are part of the standard curriculum and are required in middle school. Narrative essays are part of our curriculum during the first term of the school year. I narrow it down to a personal narrative that can provide crucial insight into a student's experiences. Personal narratives allow students to tell us about one important events in their lives—sometimes good, sometimes traumatic. They also allow us to hear their voice through the narrative's dialogue. Again, this provides an opportunity to build trust with a student.

During the third term, argumentative essays are part of our curriculum. One year, I learned firsthand how vulnerable students choose to be when they know they are in a safe environment. One particular student chose to write an essay on the death penalty. This student chose to take the side that the death penalty is an appropriate punishment for heinous murders. I conference with students to monitor their writing progress before they begin the peer-review step.

As I began reading the essay, I was preparing to make some suggestions but stopped myself. After rereading certain parts of the argument, I realized this was more than just an argumentative essay. This was an essay looking for an explanation as to why the person who shot and killed someone did not receive the death penalty. I asked the student if this was a personal story but explained that they did not have to answer that question if they felt uncomfortable. The student's head dropped, and they began describing the events that surrounded a murder of a family member. My heart broke as the student asked for an explanation. (Prior to teaching, I spent nearly ten years in law enforcement, many of those years working cases similar to this, so students were aware of my background).

Sometimes, no words can help, and in this case, words of understanding and empathy were the only appropriate responses. This student wanted feedback, but I did not feel having this discussion in the middle of class would be appropriate in the event the student was not comfortable having this discussion in earshot of the entire class. I asked the student to come back to meet with me one-on-one during the lunch period and explained my experience working cases, even one death penalty case, and how difficult this could be on the surviving family members. We discussed the details that the student wanted to share. Again, even with years of experience in law enforcement, there are times when I am left speechless. The courage and strength this student demonstrated spoke volumes about their support system.

The final draft of this essay was very well written and told a compelling story. This student was an exceptional writer, so not much editing was needed. I did, however, tell the student how impressed I was with the strength and courage it took to write an essay on such a sensitive and personal topic. I told the student that I hoped one day they would be able to share this story with others because so many young people would benefit from their strength and courage to write about such a difficult topic.

A Lasting Impact

One year, I was packing things up for summer in my classroom when two of my former students came through my door. At first, I was speechless and could not imagine how these two young men had gone from two students who tried me at every turn during my first year to those who stood before me. They hugged me and explained that they came back that day, the day after their graduation, to tell me that I was one of the few people in their lives who always believed in them, even when they did not believe in themselves. They said they remembered I told them I knew they would be successful and wanted them to come back one day to tell me just how well their lives were going. We laughed as we reminisced about some events that transpired that year. They said their eighth-grade year was one of the best years of their school careers. They both said that the encouragement I provided and the way I made them work hard helped them during their four years of high school. On this day, I could not have been prouder as they both told me of their successes and what their next steps would be. One was headed to a university in Virginia to study forensics, and the other was already working on his EMT license, planning to become a firefighter.

One of those two boys had emailed me several times throughout high school with updates and pictures of his life. This is an excerpt from one of those emails:

> *Hey Mrs. Porter*
>
> *I was just emailing you to tell you how these two years of high school have been. Where do I start? They haven't been a breeze, I can tell you that. The first year was difficult not having you there to help me through it and through class like you always did. I got behind and got down a credit plus Coronavirus, so I didn't even really get to finish my freshman year and get the full experience, but I finished it on virtual. It definitely took some getting used to. I'm still getting used to it, but I'm getting the hang of it. My sophomore year hasn't been all butterflies and rainbows either, but I'm making it through.*
>
> *I hope those kids aren't treating you badly. You're one of the best teachers I've ever had.*
>
> *I miss you as my teacher a lot. You helped me out so much, and I would not have made it to high school without you. We plan on visiting you next year, and I didn't want to wait to reach out. After all, you were like a school mom to me.*
>
> *That's how life's been treating me.*
>
> *P.S. I would have written sooner if I knew where to start.*

This lasting impact shines brightly through emails or letters students write as they move on to the next educational phase in their lives. Students email me throughout their high school years; they come by my classroom to visit throughout the school year, and even call their siblings in my class and ask to speak with me. Knowing I made an impact in their lives helps me realize my *WHY*. Even though I was *their* teacher, they have taught *me* about patience, kindness, strength, courage, and resilience.

References

Brooks, C. F., & Young, S. L. (2011). Are choice-making opportunities needed in the classroom? Using self-determination theory to consider student motivation and learner empowerment. *International Journal of Teaching and Learning in Higher Education*, *23*(1), 48–59.

Chafouleas, S. M., Johnson, A. H., Overstreet, S., & Santos, N. M. (2016). Toward a blueprint for trauma-informed service delivery in schools. *School Mental Health*, *8*, 144–162.

Crouch, E., Probst, J. C., Radcliff, E., Bennett, K. J., & McKinney, S. H. (2019). Prevalence of adverse childhood experiences (ACEs) among US children. *Child abuse & neglect*, *92*, 209–218.

Darling-Hammond, L., & DePaoli, J. (2020). Why school climate matters and what can be done to improve it. *State Education Standard*, *20*(2), 7.

Lebrun-Harris, L. A., Ghandour, R. M., Kogan, M. D., & Warren, M. D. (2022). Five-year trends in US children's health and well-being, 2016-2020. *JAMA pediatrics*, *176*(7), e220056-e220056.

Murphey, D., & Sacks, V. (2019). Supporting students with adverse childhood experiences: How educators and schools can help. *American Educator*, *43*(2), 8–11.

Platt, J. (2018). How far does choice theory succeed, within classics, as a form of differentiation in the classroom? *Journal of Classics Teaching*, *19*(37), 10–16.

Sacks, V., & Murphey, D. (2018). The prevalence of adverse childhood experiences, nationally, by state, and by race or ethnicity. *Child trends*, *20*, 2018.

Smith, D., Frey N., Pumpian, I., & Fisher, D. (2017). *Building equity: Policies and practices to empower all learners*. ASCD.

US Department of Education. (2021). *Supporting child and student social, emotional, behavioral, and mental health needs*. https://www.ed.gov/sites/ed/files/documents/students/supporting-child-student-social-emotional-behavioral-mental-health.pdf

Walter, S. M., Lambie, G. W., & Ngazimbi, E. E. (2008). A choice theory counseling group succeeds with middle school students who displayed disciplinary problems. *Middle School Journal*, *40*(2), 4–12.

CHAPTER 6

Creating Equity with Secondary Students Who Have Experienced Personal or Community Trauma by Using a Bifocal Perspective

KEONA GRIFFIN-KING

IN THE LATE 20TH century, educators' reactions to students who acted out or disrupted instruction largely relied on a disciplinary structure that removed students from the classroom and sometimes resulted in suspension or expulsion (Gowdey, 2015). These practices contributed to what became known as the school-to-prison pipeline, where a disproportionate number of students with disabilities, those who lived in poverty, and non-white students were removed from the classroom and (in some cases) placed in a juvenile justice system that was ill-equipped to truly understand why these students had acted out, thus causing even more trauma (Gowdey, 2015).

Traditionally, teachers have tended to *react* to students' misbehaviors as if the students could and should control their actions regardless of the root cause (Gross, 2020). These *reactions* have often resulted in disruptions to the learning process, students being sent out of the classroom, thus missing valuable instruction, or even worse, students being suspended or expelled from school, which puts them at risk of academic failure and even possibly ending up interacting with the juvenile justice system (Gowdey, 2015; Gross, 2020).

Within the last decade, however, more and more school districts have offered professional development on trauma-informed practices. These trainings are helping educators become aware of *why* students act out—that the adverse childhood experiences students may have experienced can be the sources of triggers, which can manifest in a variety of negative actions (Korpics et al., 2021; McIntyre et al., 2019). It is when teachers begin to ask *why* students are acting out that they can take a step back and attempt to view students' behaviors through a bifurcated perspective. Educators who consider that students' actions might be a manifestation of an adverse experience (one which occurred in the past, a complex set of traumatic experiences, or toxic stress) (Korpics et al., 2021) are, in essence, putting on what we might refer to as *trauma bifocals*. These bifocals allow them to see what is in close proximity (the student's actions) and what may be further away or unclear at the moment (the true reason behind the actions).

The Bifocal Metaphor

When our vision is impaired, glasses allow us to see more clearly. This is important for students who have experienced trauma and are triggered at school, as they are operating from their survival brain. This is the oldest part of the brain, containing the limbic region—amygdala, hypothalamus, and brain stem—and contributes to the activation of the sympathetic nervous system or the body's fight-or-flight response (Siegel, 2010). When this system is activated, the student is locked out of their upstairs brain, which is responsible for higher-order thinking and learning (Keels et al., 2021), and they can act out or act impulsively. Kim and Choi (2020) note that childhood trauma and PTSD symptoms contribute to impulsivity. When students impulsively act out, teachers who are not approaching these situations through a trauma-informed (bifocal) lens often rely on more traditional disciplinary measures.

A teacher who views these situations through a bifocal lens will be able to see through the impulsive acts and begin to ask why a student is acting out rather than simply reacting to the student's misbehavior. Without our trauma bifocals, we may see only the outward expression of internal stress and turmoil. Often, traumatized students have little control over their actions, as their bodies are on autopilot, trying to figure out how to stay safe and survive (Kim & Choi, 2020; Siegel, 2010). This incomplete image and subsequent lack of knowledge may lead teachers to make decisions that may not be in the student's best interest during a potentially critical time and may further traumatize or retraumatize the student (Cox et al., 2017; Venet, 2021).

Surveying the reasons for a student's actions will help teachers see them and their behaviors completely and as they are—separate from each other. The dysregulated behavior that disrupts the learning environment is a form of communication, not a reflection of the student's personality or character (Smith et al., 2017; Sun & Shek, 2012). Bifocals will help the teacher with this; they will aid them in seeing the person and the deeper cues and clues to their behavior.

A Conversation at a Basketball Game Leads to a Case Study

The following case study has been used several times to help educators and high school principals bifurcate their perspectives and develop strategies for disruptive student behavior. Each time, the goal has been to help the adults see the student behind or beneath the behavior; this purview can lead to better insight and understanding, which are critical for developing discipline strategies, especially for traumatized students (McInerney & McKlindon, 2014).

The Initial Conversation

The case study was born during a conversation at a high school basketball game. The principal shared with a colleague how ineffective his discipline strategies had been in redirecting a student's behavior (Student B in the following case study). The colleague offered a hypothetical description of another type of student (Student A in the following case study) to provide a wider scope to view the challenge. The colleague asked the principal about strategies he would use for the hypothetical student. The strategies shared were very different from those tried for the real student. The colleague then revealed that there was no hypothetical student. Both students were the same person. The colleague gave that principal a pair of bifocals, a way to separate the student from their actions.

Prior to that moment, the principal had been reacting to what he saw on the surface with that student, the unwanted and disruptive behavior. The knowledge of the student's trauma history, or backstory, provided new insight that changed how the principal understood and engaged with the student. Ultimately, he would use the trauma bifocals when developing strategies for disciplining and redirecting his challenging students.

A Graduate Course Assignment

This case was further developed for a graduate-level culturally responsive teaching course assignment. A vignette was added to the student descriptions and presented to two non-Black educators as an immersive learning experience. One educator identified as male, while the other identified as female. They were first given information about Student A and asked how they would engage this student in learning and interact with this student in class. They were then presented with Student B and asked the same questions.

Both educators had very visceral reactions to the students in the case study. One felt sympathy, while the other felt empathy for Student A. Both were very interested in providing help and support to this student. Both educators had very different reactions to Student B. They were uncertain about how to engage Student B in learning. They also displayed signs of discomfort that matched their statements about being leery or apprehensive about how to approach this student. They agreed that Student B was most likely a Black male. When the graduate students learned that Student A and Student B were the same student, a rich discussion full of humble *a-ha* moments ensued around the importance of knowing a student's trauma backstory.

A Research Protocol for Data Collection

With knowledge of the impact of the bifocal lens approach for Student A and Student B, the case study was used as a data collection protocol in 2023 for this author's dissertation. In this research, secondary teachers across the Midwest US were given the following vignette and scenarios about Student A and Student B.

> **Vignette**
>
> You are a first-year teacher. You have been hired to teach at a high school in a low-income, underperforming school district. Today is your first day at your new school. It is mid-semester, and the class you will teach has had several substitutes over the past two years. Because your onboarding process has been drastically condensed

due to the immediate need to get a permanent teacher in this position, you have not reviewed the files of any of your students yet. As you are touring the building with your mentor teacher, she gives you information about the courses you will be teaching and some of the students you have encountered along the way to your classroom. The following case studies are information that resonated with you about the students.

Student A

Student A has poor attendance and mediocre grades. They could be a better student if they applied themselves more and were at school more consistently. This student is the only child, and the mother died suddenly one day while the student was at school. The student was eight years old at the time. The aunt, who is the current guardian, gave this student the bad news in the principal's office. The student never returned to the mom's home again. Student A has no relationship with their dad. The student is often sad and can't seem to get a break in life. Last semester, this student went on a family outing with a cousin and their only uncle. When they returned home, the uncle committed suicide via a pistol to the head right in front of them both.

Student B

Student B is a class clown, is often disruptive, and has several discipline referrals. This student often gets into altercations with other students and has been suspended several times for fighting or inappropriate school conduct, for example, engaging in sexual acts and having weapons and/or drug paraphernalia. The student is very popular and is often seen walking the halls and disturbing other classes. This student rarely turns in any work and is failing several courses. There are rumors about the student being involved in neighborhood gangs. This student is friends with a group of students who have similar behaviors. The student is just returning to school from a ten-day suspension for a large fight that resulted in a shoot-out at last Saturday's football game.

The vignette and case study scenarios were used as part of the larger study that sought to discover if high school teachers would alter the way they spoke to and about traumatized students if they knew their trauma backstories. Ultimately, the answer was yes; however, this yes does not stand on its own. The language teachers use to speak to and about traumatized students does not change singularly because of knowledge of students' backstories. It changes when teachers use their bifocals to (1) build relationships with students, (2) advocate for students, and (3) build equity with students in the classroom (Griffin-King, 2023). The remainder of this chapter shares study data and strategies across these three domains to further demonstrate the benefit of using a bifocal lens to see students' trauma backstories.

Using Bifocals to Build Relationships with Students

When these secondary teachers in the study were asked how they would engage with Students A and B, they shared about the importance of relationships, safety, and boundaries:

> "I would talk to Student A about something other than the class to try and establish a relationship with the student and figure out their personality and likes and dislikes."
>
> "I would work to get to know Student B and establish safety in my room with boundaries that will be firm but can be adjusted. In getting to know the student, I'll listen and try to find a way to connect and relate. The boundaries might be different for this kid."

Building relationships involves knowing, understanding, and connecting with students to create a classroom culture of mutual understanding between students and teachers (Blitz et al., 2020). Additionally, how teachers view attaining and maintaining power, control, and classroom management shifts when there are relationships (Fidyk, 2019). Old power struggles can be transformed into agency, collaboration, and intervention, and language becomes intentional and influential (Cook-Sather, 2020). The high school teachers in this study had the following to say about building relationships:

> "Building a trusting student-teacher relationship will come before anything else."

> "I have to build a relationship with them and build a rapport to understand who they are, their background, and their culture."

Building relationships with their students helped these high school teachers get to know students differently and empowered them to reframe understandings, increase tolerances, formulate new considerations, identify and recognize behavioral and emotional anomalies through body language and other nonverbal cues, and create opportunities to learn of their students' traumas or backstories (Griffin-King, 2023).

These teachers changed their perspective and language due to the study. Before, the participants framed student outbursts with the question of: *What is wrong with this student?* After participating in the research, their perspectives were bifurcated so that they could ask instead: *What happened to this student before this outburst?* They also realized that verbal and nonverbal language were essential to classroom culture, especially with regard to triggers and outbursts. Finally, they felt that tone and delivery were paramount when redirecting students' behaviors.

Using Bifocals to Advocate for Students

With the aid of bifocals, the high school teachers could see students holistically as they became aware of their backstories. Establishing rapport helped them develop empathy toward their students and their respective plights and demonstrate positive regard for their lives as students and their lives outside the classroom, as shown in these teachers' quotes:

> "We need to see students individually and make sure they know you see them."

> "I say to my students: 'It's not about right or wrong but how you deal with life right now, how to fix it. Take this lesson and apply it outside of this class.'"

> "High school students have tough choices ahead of them, and it's important to acknowledge that. I tell my students, 'Whatever you

decide to do with your life, you are still going to be one of my favorite people. We are still going to be cool; just everybody has to make different decisions.'"

Bifocals Bring Context to Dysregulated Students

Most importantly, the bifocals provided significant context for behaviors when students are dysregulated. This new knowledge and perspective reframed how teachers thought about students and unfolded through five stages. See Table 6.1 for these stages, along with supporting data from the high school teachers participating in the study.

Table 6.1
Using Bifocals to Create a Shift in Engagement

Stage	Shift	Outcome and Supporting Data
Stage One	Lens Shift *See the student, not the trauma*	Teachers no longer saw the student as the enemy who destroys their learning environment and makes their job difficult: "Their intelligence is hidden behind the trauma."
Stage Two	Recognition Shift *See through the behavior*	Teachers recognized the behavior as communication rather than a personal attack: "If you have insight into a student's situation, you are able to cater to what they need a little bit more. but I think my biggest takeaway is you have to see through the behavior."
Stage Three	Language Shift *Confidence in talking with other colleagues*	Teachers' language became more intentional and focused on the behavior, not the student as a person with flaws. "But one thing I think I can confidently do is after listening to others vent about an interaction with a student, I am going to bring it back to understanding the student and the reason for their behavior."
Stage Four	Response Shift *Creating restorative consequences for students*	Teachers elicited responses from understanding instead of reactions from blaming or confusion. Instead of writing referrals for students who acted out, this teacher would use his relationship to redirect their behavior and write an incident report for the office. "That way the school would have a record but would know that further disciplinary action was not necessary."
Stage Five	Engagement Shift *Be the bridge for students*	Teachers were able to transform how they engaged when students are dysregulated. "Play your part and then make sure you're the bridge not the gap between the student and additional help."

Not only did these high school teachers' new language reflect their new understandings, but it also influenced how students saw themselves and how other teachers saw the students. Classroom culture evolved language into help and support when teachers were made aware that trauma or adverse childhood experiences were present in a student's history.

Using Bifocals to Create Equity with Students

It's hard to accept that examples like Student A and Student B reflect students' real lives, especially when they go against what we consider *normal*. The truth is, when life happens to some students, we often don't realize just how deep their stress and trauma run. As Dr. Steven Silver notes, school is meant to be a safe space for students (Wolpow et al., 2016). If we want schools to be equitable, they need to be equitable for all students, including those dealing with trauma. This might mean that adults need to be mindful of their words and actions to avoid adding to the toxic stress or retraumatizing these students. Dr. Silver refers to this as sanctuary trauma (Bloom, 2013; Figley, 2014). When educators respond to traumatized students with understanding, we can help reduce the negative impact of their experiences and create a positive, safe, and fair learning environment.

If schools were as intentional about protecting and dignifying students' trauma histories as they are with their abilities, religion, gender identity, and sexual orientation, we could start to see students through a truly equitable lens, balancing how we perceive and address behavior (Venet, 2021). Schools must first understand that trauma is an essential equity characteristic, much like culture, socioeconomic status, gender identity, or refugee status. Recognizing trauma as an equity issue is critical because many students have experienced at least one adverse childhood or community experience (Ellis & Dietz, 2017; Smith et al., 2017; Venet, 2021). Children's brains continue to develop into their early twenties, and as previously discussed in this chapter, trauma activates the survival part of their brain (Siegel, 2010). When this part is triggered, students respond in ways that can easily be misinterpreted as misbehavior. This misunderstanding leads to harmful consequences and actions that can add to the student's trauma (Oostdam et al., 2019).

Schools can integrate trauma awareness into their culture by creating campaigns that highlight the most common traumas within their specific communities. Involve students in raising awareness, creating safe spaces for conversations, and offering peer support, while providing immediate and accessible resources. These steps will help reduce stigma, remind students they're not alone, and empower them.

In terms of how we discuss and present student behavior, schools can include this information in their student management systems, with the appropriately needed safeguards and an established process to gain permission to access that information. Encourage teachers and administrators to create a system to gather and share this information with colleagues and stakeholders. When we think about universal design and equity in schools, trauma must be part of the conversation alongside other ways we identify and classify students. We need to provide learning opportunities for pre-service and certified teachers on trauma and classroom management so they can effectively support students.

References

Blitz, L. V., Yull, D., & Clauhs, M. (2020). Bringing sanctuary to school: Assessing school climate as a foundation for culturally responsive trauma-informed approaches for urban schools. *Urban Education, 55*(1), 94–124. https://doi.org/10.1177/0042085916651323

Bloom, S. L. (2013). *Creating sanctuary: Toward the evolution of sane societies.* Routledge.

Cook-Sather, A. (2020). Student voice across contexts: Fostering student agency in today's schools. *Theory Into Practice, 59*(2), 182–191. https://doi.org/https;//10.1080/00405841.2019.1705091

Cox, G., Arnold, K., Krummer, T. R., & Mccullough, D. (2017). *Hand in hand: A manual for creating trauma-informed leadership committees.* Beyond Consequences Institute, LLC.

Ellis, W. R., & Dietz, W. H. (2017). A new framework for addressing adverse childhood and community experiences: The building community resilience model. *Academic Pediatrics,17*(7S), S86–S93.

Fidyk, A. (2019). Trauma-sensitive practices for new teacher standards: Addressing the epidemic of our times. *In Education, 25*(1), 51–76.

Figley, C. R. (Ed.). (2014). *Trauma and its wake.* Routledge.

Gowdey, L. J. (2015). Disabling discipline: Locating a right to representation of students with disabilities in the ADA. *Columbia Law Review, 115*, 2265-2309.

Griffin-King, K. N. (2023) *How backstories influence the way teachers speak to and about traumatized students: A case study.* All Theses, Dissertations, and Capstone Projects. 664. https://griffinshare.fontbonne.edu/all-etds/664

Gross, K. (2020). *Trauma doesn't stop at the school door: Strategies and solutions for educators, PreK–college.* Teachers College Press.

Keels, M., Dinizulu, S., Parikh, S., & Jointer, T. (2021). Preparing schools to meet the needs of students coping with trauma and toxic stress. Brief No. 17. *EdResearch for Recovery Project.*

Kim, J. H., & Choi, J. Y. (2020). Influence of childhood trauma and post-traumatic stress symptoms on impulsivity: Focusing on differences according to the dimensions of impulsivity. *European Journal of Psychotraumatology*, *11*(1), Article 1796276. https://doi.org/10.1080/20008198.2020.1796276

Korpics, J., Altman, L., Feinglass, J., & Stillerman, A. (2021). Prevalence and impact of adverse childhood experiences on Chicago public school students in the youth risk behavior survey. *Journal of School Health*, *91*(10), 802–812.

McInerney, M., & McKlindon, A. (2014). Unlocking the door to learning: Trauma-informed classrooms & transformational schools. *Education Law Center*, 1–24.

McIntyre, E. M., Baker, C. N., Overstreet, S., & The New Orleans Trauma-Informed Schools Learning Collaborative. (2019). Evaluating foundational professional development training for trauma-informed approaches in schools. *Psychological Services, 16*(1), 95–102. https://doi.org/10.1037/ser0000312

Oostdam, R. J., Koerhuis, M. J., & Fukkink, R. G. (2019). Maladaptive behavior in relation to the basic psychological needs of students in secondary education. *Eur J. Psychologic Education, 34*, 601–619.

Siegel, D. J. (2010). *Mindsight: The new science of personal transformation*. Bantam.

Smith, D., Frey, N., Pumpian, I., & Fisher, D. (2017). *Building equity: Policies and practices to empower all learners*. ASCD.

Sun, R. C., & Shek, D. T. (2012). Student classroom misbehavior: An exploratory study based on teachers' perceptions. *The Scientific World Journal*, *2012*(1), 1–8. https://doi.org/10.1100/2012/208907

Venet, A. S. (2021). *Equity-centered trauma-informed education*. W. W. Norton & Co.

Wolpow, R., Johnson, M. M., Hertel, R., & Kincaid, S. O. (2016). *The heart of learning and teaching: Compassion, resiliency, and academic success* (3rd ed.). Washington State Office of Superintendent of Public Instruction.

CHAPTER 7

"If My Teacher Had Known"—College Students' Reflective Perceptions about Sharing Challenging Events with Middle or High School Teachers

JOANNE FISH AND JAMIE DORONKIN

Introduction

CURRENT RESEARCH AND LITERATURE confirm that, in general, the well-being of children has worsened over time, and many adolescents experience some form of a traumatic event, toxic stress, or complex trauma that develops from community or social trauma (Crouch et al., 2019; Finkelhor, 2020; Sacks & Murphey, 2018). However, as has been noted elsewhere in this book, it can be challenging to describe the state of mental health among adolescents because of the many factors contributing to their development, the complicated nature of their social interactions, and the complexity of attempting to define how individuals experience trauma. After a systematic review of various studies, Wickström and Lindholm (2020) concluded that because adolescents have varying perceptions of mental health and "mental ill-health" Hellström & Beckman, 2021, p. 1, distinguishing between mental health challenges and everyday challenges is complex (Hellström & Beckman, 2021). Adding to this are the challenges for early adolescents that revolve around social development, including being seen and accepted for who they are, all while navigating cognitive changes and emotional shifts that include forming and maintaining trusting relationships apart from their family of origin (Frydman & Mayor, 2017; Tucker et al., 2011).

Whether adolescents experience a singular trauma event, complex persistent stress such as living in poverty, or simply the challenges that are a natural part of being an adolescent, connecting with teachers is often noted as a source of support (Smith et al., 2017). On the other hand, some adolescents may not feel comfortable initiating these kinds of connections, and risk feeling isolated (Anda et al., 2010; Bremner, 2006; Centers for Disease Control and Prevention, 2019). Given this, we wanted to gain insight into how adolescents perceived the possibilities of reaching out to teachers when they experienced challenges. Rather than survey or interview adolescents, we sought to understand how adults reflected (Nardon et al., 2021) on the challenges they faced during their adolescent years in middle and high school. This chapter presents the findings and implications of a study that examined the reflective premise of "If my teacher had known."

Research Study Aim

To gather reflective data about adolescents' experiences of reaching out to teachers for support within the premise of "If my teacher had known..." we recruited college students from the university's College of Education to participate in our study. We designed an online survey with four open-ended questions (see Table 7.1) that asked students to reflect on challenges they may have experienced in middle or high school and what they remembered about sharing those challenges with their teachers during those years. Our original intention was to recruit students from the entire university student body, but even with Institutional Review Board approval, permission from the Provost was only granted to recruit from the College of Education.

Four study queries of (1) anticipated sharing, (2) anticipated impact, (3) actual impact, and (4) teacher actions and dispositions guided the development of the open-ended survey questions. See Table 7.1 for the relationship between the study's queries and data sources.

Table 7.1
Study Queries and Data Sources

Study Queries	Data Sources: Open-Ended Survey Questions
Anticipated Sharing	Thinking back on your middle and high school years, if you could have shared with your teachers about challenges you were experiencing, what would those be?
Teacher Actions or Dispositions	If there were teachers during your middle and high school years that you were able to share challenges with, what helped you to know that you could share with them?
Anticipated Impact on Learning	If your teachers had known about those challenges, how do you believe that would have impacted your learning experiences?
Actual Impact on Learning	If you did share challenges with your teacher, do you believe sharing had an impact on your learning? If so, in what ways?

Participant Demographics

We were able to recruit 24 college students to participate in the study. The ages of the participants ranged from 18 to mid-30s, with 75% (*n* = 18) between 18 and 23. The majority of participants (67%) identified as female (*n* = 16), and (33%) identified as male (*n* = 8). Most of the college students (71%) were white (*n* = 17), three participants were Black, three participants were Asian, and one participant was Native Hawaiian. When asked if they received free or reduced lunches during middle or high school, 71% (*n* = 17) of participants responded with "no," while 25% (*n* = 6) responded with "yes," and one participant was unsure. Most of the college students in this study were white, identified as female, were between 18 and 23 years old, and did not receive free or reduced lunches during middle or high school, which aligns with the demographics of teachers and teacher candidates in the United States (Goings et al., 2018).

Research Methodology

The decision to use reflective surveys rather than surveying adolescents of middle and high school age was both practical and theoretical. We knew that getting permission from local schools and parents of underage participants would prove to be difficult, especially given the time frame in which we had to work. Theoretically, we borrowed from the framework of reflective interviewing developed by Nardon et al. (2021). This framework combines knowledge gained from literature about using interviews as interventions and reflection couched in transformative learning theory (Nardon et al., 2021). While this framework is focused on interviewing and not surveys, we felt that it was easily applied, considering that our surveys employed open-ended questions that allowed participants ample opportunities to reflect.

Nardon et al.'s (2021) framework is based on four principles: 1. Give participants time to think; 2. Develop a relationship of trust; 3. Invite reflection; and 4. Support the identification of solutions. We argue that we were able to honor these principles by our research methods and survey designs (see Table 7.2). Note that these principles are not meant to be linear or in any way chronological.

Table 7.2
Principles of Reflective Research and Study Design

Principles of Reflective Research	**Study Design Elements**
Give participants time to think	The use of open-ended questions allowed ample opportunity for participants to reflect on and convey those reflective memories.
Develop a relationship of trust	Within the informed consent form, we ensured that participants would have anonymity. Participants were asked to volunteer, and all surveys were collected electronically, ensuring anonymity. Other than gathering some demographic information, all other questions were open-ended and allowed participants to provide as few or as many details as they wished.
Invite reflection	We used phrases that invited reflective thinking, such as: *thinking back* *if you could have shared* *what would those* *if your teachers had known* *do you believe* *if there were* *what helped*
Support the identification of solutions	Our questions supported thinking that allowed our participants to reflect beyond the challenges they were remembering and think about their perceptions of the impact of sharing those challenges.

Data Analysis

Study data were analyzed using an inductive/deductive hybrid thematic analysis process (Fereday & Muir-Cochrane, 2006; Proudfoot, 2023). One of us used deductive coding using the study queries, as noted in Table 7.1, and the other inductively coded for organically occurring and emerging content (Burkholder et al., 2020). The thematic analysis process included prolonged engagement with the data, incorporating the iterative process of open and axial coding, and the selective grouping of data codes into themes (Creswell & Poth, 2018). We were also guided by a triangulation process that included coding frameworks, vetting codes and themes, peer debriefing, and theoretical and literature consensus (Nowell et al., 2017).

The themes that emerged from the analysis allowed us to further organize the study queries into those concerning social-emotional well-being and those concerning learning or academic well-being (see Table 7.3). Each theme, along with its supporting theoretical frameworks and data, will be explored next.

Table 7.3
Study Queries and Themes

Study Queries	Themes
Impact on Social-Emotional Wellbeing	
Anticipated Sharing	Family Struggles Self-Esteem Issues Life Balance
Teacher Actions or Dispositions	Safety Listening Connection
Impact on Learning	
Anticipated Impact	Equity Compassion No Help
Actual Impact	Perceived lack of impact on learning Compartmentalization of trauma/challenges and learning

Connecting Findings with Currently Accepted Theoretical Frameworks

Central to the themes generated by our data is the idea that student-teacher relationships are key to students' perceptions of feeling supported. Based on students' responses, we noticed that from the students' perspectives, their teachers operationalized compassion and caring by listening, creating safe spaces (both physical and abstract), and making and allowing space for connections. Participants' responses illustrated the extent to which students value these relationships, as discovered in statements such as, "They seemed open and interested in listening and learning about me and who I am as a person and not just as a student," and "They reached out to make a connection with me."

These findings are consistent with previous studies situated around various relationship theories. For example, our participants echoed the argument made by Bayram Özdemir and Özdemir (2020), which posits that students seek supportive and fair relationships with their teachers. This argument is based on several theoretical frameworks, such as attachment theory (Bowlby, 1969), social-motivation theories, such as self-determination theory (Deci & Ryan, 2000) and belonging theories (Dearth-Wesley et al., 2023; Faircloth & Hamm, 2005; Wang & Degol, 2016).

Attachment and Social Motivation Theories

Attachment theory (Bowlby, 1969) is often noted in studies relating to early childhood and elementary students, which postulates that when students form close relationships with teachers, they feel secure. This, in turn, fosters a student's positive sense of self, paving the way for a willingness to explore and motivation to learn.

Social motivation theories focus on students' basic psychological needs, such as a sense of belonging and connectedness to school. This can be found in relationships with peer groups or teacher-student relationships. Students need to feel valued and have a sense of *fitting in*. Ruzek et al. (2016) describe three dimensions of teacher-student relationships regarding adolescents. These are *perceived support, utilization,* and *a sense of relatedness*. Perceived support relates to how students feel that teachers are sensitive to their needs and whether they are supportive. Utilization has to do with whether students are willing to rely on their teachers for help. A sense of relatedness refers to students' sense of belonging and acceptance. When students' psychological needs are met, and they feel connected to their teachers and school community, they are more likely to succeed academically (Jennings, 2018).

Positive student-teacher relationships can contribute to students' sense of belonging (Raufelder & Kulakow, 2022), and a sense of belonging, in turn, can be a protective factor for students who experience personal challenges (Korpershoek et al., 2020). When students feel as if they belong, they feel that they are important members of their school communities, but more importantly, they feel supported (Goodenow & Grady, 1993). This idea that they are a *part* of the larger community allows them to have the self-confidence they need to be both socially and academically successful (Goodenow & Grady, 1993; Korpersoek et al., 2020).

Social Support Frameworks

While our study is connected to both attachment theory and social motivation theory, the theoretical framework that we feel our findings best align with is that of *social support*. In this framework, students view support from teachers as a personal resource that can act as a "buffer against the challenges students may face" (Bayram Özdemir & Özdemir, 2020, p. 922). This framework considers three main dimensions of support: informational, instrumental, and emotional (Wentzel, 2004) (see Table 7.4)

Another support framework to consider is that of Bostwick et al. (2022). These researchers from New South Wales, Australia conducted a longitudinal study that "examined the reciprocal relationships among students' academic buoyancy, their perceptions of school support (learning support, teacher relational support, school belonging, and classroom management), and their motivation and engagement (perseverance, perceived competence, valuing of school) across one year of school" (p. 1931). This large study (N = 71,681 secondary students in grades 7–11) found that in schools where students felt a sense of school belonging, there was a higher average academic buoyancy a year later. The authors defined academic buoyancy as "students' capacity to manage everyday setbacks and challenges at school" (p. 1931). The types of support Bostwick et al. (2022) considered were: *learning support, teacher relational support, school belonging, and classroom management* (see Table 7.4).

Table 7.4
Student-Perceived Dimensions of Support from Teachers

Dimensions of Support (Wentzel, 2004)	Description of students' perceptions of support from teachers
Informational	Students' perception of receiving clear guidance on what is expected and valued in the classroom
Instrumental	Students' perception of getting needed help and advice from teachers
Emotional	Students' perception that their relationships with teachers are nurturing and emotionally supportive
Type of Support (Bostwick et al., 2022)	**Description of students' perceptions of support from teachers**
Learning support	"perceptions of academic support received from teachers, such as the extent to which teachers were interested in students' academic progress and learning in school" (p. 1934)
Teacher relational support	"students' perceptions of the extent to which teachers treated students fairly, cared for them as people, and were attentive to students' needs" (p. 1934)
School belonging	"the extent to which students felt a sense of community and belonging within their school and with their peers" (p. 1934)
Classroom management	"students' perceptions of structures, rules, and behavioral expectations in the classroom" (p. 1934)

Regardless of the defined framework or lens through which to consider support types, it is clear that academic inquiries have demonstrated that when students perceive they are receiving support from their teachers and when they perceive that support as a buffer against any challenges they are facing, "they tend to be better at dealing with challenges, and in turn, have better social and academic adjustment" (Bayram Özdemir & Özdemir, 2020, p. 922). Our findings clearly support that notion.

Study Findings in Connection with Social Support Frameworks

In Tables 7.5, 7.6, and 7.7 we categorize participants' statements based on the types of support in which they best align, based on Wentzel's (2004) and Bostwick et al.'s (2022) social support frameworks. Our conclusions were derived by asking: What type of support was the student seeking by making that statement? For example, one participant noted: "*My brother struggled with anger issues and was very violent. It made it hard to be at home.*" We determined that *had* the participant shared with a teacher, they might have been seeking advice on how to navigate their home life, aligning this statement with the instrumental dimension (Wentzel, 2004) or teacher relational support (Bostwick et al., 2022). Additionally, we felt the student was hoping for understanding and support from their teacher, categorizing the statement as an *emotional dimension* of support.

Study Query: Anticipated Sharing of Challenges

Identified Themes: Family Struggles, Self-Esteem Issues, and Life Balance Challenges

We asked students what they would have shared if they had felt comfortable sharing with their teachers. Students indicated they would have shared about their family struggles, self-esteem issues, and school-life balance challenges. These were all very personal experiences or situations, and if students had felt as if they could share them, the learners thought it might have helped them feel more at ease at school. While some of their experiences could be classified as trauma events, most seemed to fit more aptly in the category of toxic stress. The Center on the Developing Child of Harvard University (2024) defines toxic stress as "excessive or prolonged activation of stress response systems in the body and brain" (para. 1). It seems that most of the experiences our participants described resulted in a toxic stress response. A toxic stress response is a "prolonged activation of stress response systems in the absence of protective relationships" (para. 3).

Table 7.5
Struggles at Home — Comments Categorized by Support Type

Participants' Statements	Wentzel's (2004) Dimensions of Support	Bostwick et al.'s, (2022) Types of Support
"That my grandmother had cancer and how it was hard for my mother to juggle that alongside raising me and my sister."	emotional	teacher relational support
"Our family issues at the time and my dad had multiple surgeries. I had to take care of my dad which meant missing a lot of school."	emotional	teacher relational support school belonging
"That not participating does not mean that I am not paying attention or lazy. It is because I might have had a bad morning with my parents."	instrumental emotional	classroom management
"For any grade that was nearly less than perfect, I would be in trouble. I also faced many consequences at home for such little things and it caused major stress on me. I was not able to handle failure well at all, and I had very low self-confidence at the time."	informational emotional	learning support teacher relational support
"If I could've shared one thing it would have been struggling at home with one parent after losing a parent."	emotional	teacher relational support

Table 7.6
Self-Esteem Issues — Comments Categorized by Support Type

Participants' Statements	Wentzel's (2004) Dimensions of Support	Bostwick et al.'s, (2022) Types of Support
"I would have shared why I was so withdrawn in class. I struggled with social anxiety and didn't know there was a name for it at the time."	informational instrumental emotional	teacher relational support school belonging
"Wanting to be accepted by my fellow class-mates for being gay."	instrumental emotional	school belonging
"I never realized it back then, but I had pretty bad social anxiety. I also struggled with my body image, and it was quite obvious how insecure I was."	instrumental emotional	school belonging
"Their encouragement would have helped me recognize that having a learning disability is nothing to be ashamed of."	informational instrumental emotional	learning support teacher relational support school belonging

Table 7.7
Life Balance Challenge — Comments Categorized by Support Type

Participants' Statements	Wentzel's (2004) Dimensions of Support	Bostwick et al.'s, (2022) Types of Support
"I wish that they would have known that we really don't have all of the time in the world."	informational emotional	learning support teacher relational support classroom management
"More free time in exchange for completing study tasks would make me more motivated to study."	informational instrumental	school belonging
"I would have been more relaxed because I would've had more time to do stuff and focus on other things in my life."	instrumental	school belonging
"In my country, parents usually want students to spend more time studying, and if teachers can help students balance this time and communicate with parents, it can help students reduce stress."	informational instrumental	learning support teacher relational support

These responses tell us that students hoped that if they had shared their challenges, they would have received support on a personal level. They seem to be seeking some sort of emotional or relational connection with their teachers as well as learning support. To these students, school was about more than just learning. It was a place where they could go to make a connection they were not getting at home. Some students seem to have to take on tremendous responsibility (caring for an ill parent or grandparent, living up to an expectation that they had to be perfect, and possibly having to take on adult responsibilities in a single-parent household).

Adolescence is a time when learners are in flux. Not only are they experiencing many physical changes, but their social and emotional development is also often described as tumultuous. It is situated within "interactions among the environmental factors, relationships, and learning opportunities" (Darling-Hammond et al., 2020, p. 97) that adolescents are experiencing both in and out of school. Because they spend so much time at school and with peers, we cannot underestimate teachers' impact on this development. Both social and scientific research have demonstrated how intricately related the various contexts (places in which they live, play, work, and learn) of adolescents' developmental stages are. It is vital for educators to understand not only this integrated developmental system but also the part they play in it. The real and student-perceived support teachers can offer adolescents can be the difference between a student's *academic buoyancy* and failure to thrive (Bostwick et al., 2022).

Study Query: Teacher Actions or Dispositions

Identified Themes: Seeking Safety, Listening, Connection

Creating safe spaces for students is an integral element of a functional learning environment (Jennings, 2018). It is no coincidence that positive student-teacher relationships are founded on a mutual feeling of safety. Due to the inherent structure of the school-to-home time ratio, teachers tend to spend more time with students than do other care providers (even parents). This is especially true for adolescents who become more involved in school-based programming such as sports, clubs, and other extracurricular activities, spending more time with their school community than with the people in their homes. If there are signs that a student is in distress (changes in personal hygiene, absenteeism, a drop in grades, etc.) teachers are often the first to notice (Jennings, 2018).

Additionally, a sense of safety is foundational for building trust. In an academic setting, students count on teachers and other school community members to be trustworthy and sensitive to their needs to thrive. Jennings (2018) refers to this attachment to a community setting as "*social trust*" (p. 52). As these themes emerged from the study data, it became clear that students identified teachers' actions and dispositions that are imperative in relationship building and central to trauma-informed practices (see Table 7.8).

Table 7.8
Teacher Actions or Dispositions—Safety, Comments Categorized by Support Type

Participants' Statements	Wentzel's (2004) Dimensions of Support	Bostwick et al.'s (2022) Types of Support
"They made sure it was known they were a safe space and always open."	instrumental	teacher relational support
"I felt safe when I was with them because it was like they were listening and hearing what I was saying to them rather than brushing me off."	instrumental	teacher relational support
"They were honestly just there for me rather than lecturing me. I always felt safe when they told me it was okay to open up."	emotional	teacher relational support
"Whenever I visited his office, it felt like stepping into a safe haven. The atmosphere he created in his room was warm and welcoming, which made it easier for me to open up."	instrumental emotional	teacher relational support

Clearly, these students had identified certain teachers with whom they felt "safe" to share personal challenges. They reflected not only on the need to be able to go to an adult and space where they felt they could find refuge, but on how having that allowed them to express their concerns, emotions, or angst. Just knowing these safe spaces exist can be a protective factor for students (Zimmerman et al., 2013).

Another teacher disposition students mentioned was that of being listeners. Listening is considered to be an empathic action that, when perceived in a positive light by the person being listened to, can be an effective social support (Jones et al., 2019; Zimmerman et al., 2013). Empathy is an important component of culturally responsive pedagogy (Warren, 2018), which can be supportive for students experiencing challenges. Comments from our participants highlight their perceptions of being listened to at times of need, as well as the importance of this interaction (see Table 7.9).

Table 7.9
Teacher Actions or Dispositions—Listening, Comments Categorized by Support Type

Participants' Statements	Wentzel's (2004) Dimensions of Support	Bostwick et al.'s (2022) Types of Support
"They seemed open and interested in listening and learning about me and who I am as a person and not just as a student."	emotional	teacher relational support school belonging
"They were listening and hearing what I was saying."	informational instrumental	teacher relational support
"All they did was let me talk and listen."	instrumental	teacher relational support

When one considers that this type of support (teacher relational support) is relevant to nearly all these types of encounters, the benefits seem to be significant (Botswick et al., 2022). However, Jones et al. (2019) point out that the benefits of this type of support tend to be "predominantly a function of one's *perceived* support (e.g. the support a person thinks he or she has)" (Jones et al., 2019, p. 2). When teachers participate in a student-centered supportive encounter, it is important they participate in what Jones et al. refer to as "active listening" (2019):

> Active listening consists of (a) cognitive processes, such as attending, understanding, or interpreting messages; (b) affective processes, such as being motivated and energized to attend to another person; and (c) behavioral processes, such as verbally and nonverbally signaling that a message has been received and understood. (2019, p. 2)

Our participants' comments about listening seemed to indicate that they recognized those teachers whom they considered to be empathic listeners.

It is important that teachers recognize their role in this part of the teacher-student relationship because if a student seeking support perceives indifference, or that the teacher is not listening to their needs, the impact may be negative.

Making Meaningful Connections

When seeking support, students sought out teachers with whom they felt a connection (see Table 7.10). Research has long supported the idea that feeling a sense of connection to their teachers and school as a whole reaps a multitude of benefits for students and especially for adolescents who are beginning to pull away from their immediate families and spend more time with their school communities (Bostwick et al., 2022; Darling-Hammond, et al., 2020; Garcia-Moya et al., 2019). However, in an extensive review of the literature, Garcia-Moya et al. (2019) concluded that the concept of *teacher connectedness* is usually subsumed in other studies about school connectedness, and that it is important researchers begin looking at students' perceptions of how they connect with teachers. Given the number of comments we were able to categorize as teacher relational support (Bostwick et al., 2022), this concept should be studied more in depth.

Table 7.10
Teacher Actions or Dispositions—Connection, Comments Categorized by Support Type

Participants' Statements	Wentzel's (2004) Dimensions of Support	Bostwick et al.'s (2022) Types of Support
"I only opened up to one teacher in high school. She was like a mom, to be honest; she would give me advice about my challenges and situations and she would encourage me to better myself and get different perspectives."	instrumental	teacher relational support school belonging
"Teachers [whom] I felt comfortable sharing with had made personal connections with their students without overstepping."	emotional	teacher relational support
"They reached out to make a connection with me."	instrumental emotional	teacher relational support

Path to Resilience

When students feel it is safe to open up to their teachers, they are taking advantage of protective and resilience-promoting factors that are inherent in positive teacher-student relationships. Studying these factors is often done in the context of resilience theory (Zimmerman & Brenner, 2010; Zimmerman et al., 2013). According to resilience theory, resilience occurs when "environmental, social, and individual factors interrupt the trajectory from risk to pathology" (p. 1). Resilience theory is based on three models: compensatory, protective, and challenge (Zimmerman et al., 2013). Fergus and Zimmerman (2005) called these variables *promotive factors* "because they are associated with positive development and help youths overcome adversity" (p. 1). In other words, they promote resilience despite adversities.

Of the three models of resilience theory, the protective model highlights various factors in the life of an adolescent that would *interrupt* risks. One such protective factor could be that of a caring teacher who creates a safe space for students to go to and know that someone is listening. For example, one of our participants reported that they had lost a parent and had ended up living in a single-parent household. The student expressed this as something they were struggling with. Having an adult mentor, such as a teacher, to talk with could be considered one of those protective factors because it is considered a social support and would promote a positive social trust (Jennings, 2018) in the mind of the adolescent. Fergus and Zimmerman (2005) identify these promotive factors as assets or resources. Whether they are doing so consciously or not, students tend to use the resources in order to manage their own life's challenges. These relationships with their teachers (i.e., caring adults) are considered to be vital promotive resources (Zimmerman et al., 2013).

Anticipated and Actual Impact on Learning

The life challenges our participants included were both traumatic events and what could be categorized as persistent toxic stress. Toxic stress occurs when there is continued activation of the body's stress response systems and the absence of any sort of social or other buffers, such as a supportive relationship with a caring and trusted adult (Joos et al., 2019).

A plethora of research has concluded that childhood trauma and toxic stress can negatively impact learning (Shonkoff et al., 2012). In fact, this statement is so common within trauma literature that it is assumed. We know the basic science behind these statements: trauma negatively impacts brain development. Physiologically, the body's response to toxic stress is when the hypothalamic-pituitary-adrenal (HPA) axis and the sympathetic-adrenomedullary system are repeatedly or continually activated resulting in increased levels of the stress hormones cortisol, norepinephrine, and adrenaline (Shonkoff et al., 2012). These hormonal dysregulations can "disrupt developing brain architecture" (Joos et al., 2019, p. 46), especially the regions of the brain responsible for learning: the hippocampus and prefrontal cortex (National Scientific Council on the Developing Child, 2005/2014).

While the science is sound, our study findings demonstrate that the issue may be more complex than simple physiology. Promotive factors that can interrupt the damage done by toxic stress include social support systems. These support systems can include a caring, trusted adult such as a teacher who listens. Schools play a vital role in creating environments that promote social and emotional well-being, especially for students who are experiencing challenges (Maloney et al., 2024).

Today's adolescents are especially vulnerable to adversity and a number of challenges we have not seen before. They are not only navigating normal adolescent developmental angst, but they are also faced with types of challenges previous generations have not seen. They are facing the uncertainty of climate change, the often-negative impact of social media, a heightened awareness of war and global atrocities, as well as a number of inequities. These challenges have been further exacerbated by the COVID-19 pandemic, which plummeted today's adolescents into isolation, causing a number of mental health problems (Goldstein & Brooks, 2023; Maloney et al., 2024).

Equity and Compassion

A central tenet of this book involves building equity as crucial support for trauma-informed practices (Smith et al., 2017). The study findings for our anticipated impact on learning inquiry support this tenet with the themes of equity and compassion. As these themes emerged from the study data, it became apparent that students were hopeful that sharing challenges with teachers could lead to more equitable treatment and compassion, especially regarding schoolwork.

Venet (2021) makes an excellent argument that too often educators assume that being trauma-informed has to do with responding to or mitigating the trauma students bring *to* the classroom from outside school. However, as Venet argues and our participants allude to, trauma and toxic stress can easily originate from *within* the classroom or at least be exacerbated by academic expectations if teachers are not aware of or do not know how to mitigate the stressors students may be experiencing. If educators make the mistake of too narrowly defining trauma and toxic stress by insinuating the job is to help students manage those things, we are negating the possibility that we (educators) could be the unwitting initiators of those adverse experiences.

In responding to our question about what impact on learning they thought sharing challenges might have had, our participants were clearly seeking equity—a sense of fairness—given what they were attempting to navigate on their own. Judith Herman (2015), a leading expert on trauma and recovery, points out that "traumatic events are extraordinary, not because they occur rarely, but rather because they overwhelm the ordinary human adaptations to life" (p. 33). Our participants were attempting to adapt to whatever experiences they were having.

Our participants were not only seeking support but also a sense of equity. They were hoping to find ways to adapt to whatever adversities they were experiencing, but they clearly needed support from their teachers to do that. Venet (2021) argues that one path to equitable practices is for our education system to change the view of trauma-informed education from addressing it on an individualized (per student) basis to a more holistic, systemic, or structural lens. "When we recognize that social, historical, and political factors shape trauma, we can imagine ways that schools can influence these factors in pursuit of a better world" (Venet, 2021, p. 9). This becomes especially important when students sense teacher or school bias. Recent studies demonstrated that when students perceive teacher bias or unfairness, their academic success is negatively impacted (Chen & Cui, 2019; Gini et al., 2018). The comments that follow demonstrate students' desire for equity despite those students not communicating those challenges with their teachers (see Table 7.11).

Table 7.11
Anticipated Impact: A Hope for Equity, Comments Categorized by Support Type

Participants' Statements	Wentzel's (2004) Dimensions of Support	Bostwick et al.'s (2022) Types of Support
"I think if my teachers had known I would have maybe gotten appropriate resources to help me with my thoughts, feelings, and confidence."	informational instrumental emotional	learning support teacher relational support school belonging
"If my teachers had known this and cared, I believe their support would have helped me focus and feel that I belonged."	instrumental emotional	teacher relational support school belonging
"I believe that if I had ever confided in them about my learning disability, they would have responded with empathy and reassurance. I'm confident that they would have emphasized the importance of understanding and embracing the uniqueness of each individual's learning process. Their encouragement would have helped me recognize that having a learning disability is nothing to be ashamed of; rather, it's a part of what makes me who I am."	instrumental emotional	learning support teacher relational support school belonging

Anticipated Impact: Compassion Seeking

Students in this study thought they would have received more compassion from their teachers if they had been able to share their personal challenges with them. In her book, *The Trauma-Sensitive Classroom: Building Resilience with Compassionate Teaching,* Patricia Jennings (2018) discusses the three major systems we employ for our survival: the threat system, the drive system, and the affiliation or soothing system. The threat system refers to our body's physiological response to threat. This includes an activated hypothalamic-pituitary-adrenal (HPA) axis and sympathetic-adrenomedullary system resulting in our fight, flight, or flee response. The drive system has to do with us getting what we need in order to accomplish goals. The affiliation (or soothing) system involves us creating social bonds with others within our communities (families, schools, work, neighborhoods, and so forth). The affiliation system teaches us to cooperate with others in order to ensure our mutual survival, but this involves developing healthy attachments.

Students with trauma or toxic stress experiences tend to develop problems with attachment because they have not had enough healthy working relationship models (Jennings, 2018). Teachers are in unique positions to model these healthy relationships for all students. If successful, students can develop working and positive affiliation systems that can lead to their success, both socially and academically. The students in our study seemed to instinctively understand this as evident in the following statements found in Table 7.12.

Table 7.12
Anticipated Impact: Compassion Seeking, Comments Categorized by Support Type

Participants' Statements	Wentzel's (2004) Dimensions of Support	Bostwick et al.'s (2022) Types of Support
"I think that teachers might have gone easier on me. They might have reached out to see how they could help or how they could make school easier."	instrumental emotional	learning support teacher relational support
"It would have had a positive impact because I would have known the teachers cared about me other than just teaching at me."	emotional	teacher relational support school belonging
"More understanding for why I was missing classes."	emotional	teacher relational support
"Feeling like the oddball out. I was made fun of and not liked. I was a quiet student. So, if my teachers had known this and cared, I believe their support would have helped."	emotional	school belonging

Anticipated Impact on Learning: No Help—The Art of Compartmentalizing

Gaining students' trust involves many nuances. These students compartmentalized their trauma and did not connect it with their learning. Teachers need to make concerted efforts to gain trust. VanderWoude's (2024) study on teacher-student relationships and how they affect resilience found that when students perceive a level of closeness between themselves and their teachers, their level of trust increases, and they perceive higher levels of support. Trust is a significant aspect of teacher-student relationships (Bonanno et al., 2024). The Missouri Model of Trauma-Informed Approaches (MDMHP, 2019/2014)considers trustworthiness as one of its key tenets. While some of the participants in our study indicated that they had shared some of their challenges with their teachers, not all participants were convinced that doing so would have positively impacted their learning (see Table 7.13).

Table 7.13
Anticipated Impact: Negative Perceptions, Comments Categorized by Support Type

Participants' Statements	Wentzel's (2004) Dimensions of Support	Bostwick et al.'s (2022) Types of Support
"I think they would've thought the bullying was just kids messing/playing around so I do not think they would have taken it seriously."	instrumental emotional	teacher relational support
"I was already receiving support on the side to learn English, so I think that was their priority and not necessarily how I felt about this new environment or my feelings in general."	instrumental emotional	learning support teacher relational support school belonging
"Not really, because my issue was about making the world more accepting."	instrumental	teacher relational support school belonging

These results seemed puzzling at first. They seemed to contradict the literature as well as the experiences shared by other participants. However, when one takes into consideration that it is not the support that counts, but the *perceived* support that matters (Zimmerman et al., 2013), it begins to make sense. We wonder if it might be important for students to be made aware of the impact positive teacher-student relationships could have on their learning. With this in mind, we offer some thoughts on changing the dynamic.

Creating a Climate for Change

Implicit in our findings is the need for change in how our education system, as well as our educators, understand and facilitate a trauma-informed culture. Most of our participants had graduated from high school only within the previous two to three years, highlighting the current state of trauma-informed practices within our middle and high schools. While many responses illustrate that positive relationships with teachers are nurturing, helping adolescents understand the importance of sharing their challenges with a trusted adult is just as important as helping educators develop practices that provide for equity by creating trustworthiness and demonstrating compassion while creating a culture of accountability, and promoting a system of affiliation through collaboration.

This study employed a student-centered approach in which our intention was to highlight student voices. We posit that letting students in on the work of creating trauma-informed school cultures will not only build trust but will also help to create a sense of belonging among school-age students and build equity as they begin to see themselves as equal members of school communities. Letting students in on the *why* could help give teachers a voice to say, "Hey, you may feel like it doesn't matter if you tell us these things, and we know it doesn't make sense because nowhere else in your experience does it matter, but we are here to help you navigate these challenges."

Refernces

Anda, R. F., Butchart, A., Felitti, V. J., & Brown, D. W. (2010). Building a framework for global surveillance of the public health implications on adverse childhood experiences. *American Journal of Preventive Medicine, 39*(1), 93–98.

Bayram Özdemir, S., & Özdemir, M. (2020). How do adolescents' perceptions of relationships with teachers change during upper-secondary school years? *Journal of Youth and Adolescence*, *49*(4), 921–935.

Bonanno, A., Briesch, A. M., Lifter, K., & Kemerer, P. (2024). Measuring teacher-student relationships in adolescence: A systematic, cross-cultural review. *International Journal of School & Educational Psychology*, *12*(2), 96-108.

Bostwick, K. C., Martin, A. J., Collie, R. J., Burns, E. C., Hare, N., Cox, S., Flesken, A., & McCarthy, I. (2022). Academic buoyancy in high school: A cross-lagged multilevel modeling approach exploring reciprocal effects with perceived school support, motivation, and engagement. *Journal of Educational Psychology*, *114*(8), 19–31.

Bowlby, J. (1969). *Attachment and loss* (2nd ed., Vol 1.). Basic Books.

Bremner, J. D. (2006). Traumatic stress: Effects on the brain. *Dialogues in Clinical Neuroscience, 8*(4), 445–461.

Burkholder, G. J., Cox, K. A., Crawford, L. M., & Hitchcock, J. H. (Eds.). (2020). *Research design and methods: An applied guide for the scholar-practitioner*. Sage Publications.

Centers for Disease Control and Prevention. (2019, April 19). *Data statistics on children's mental health*. https://www.cdc.gov/children-mental-health/data-research/?CDC_AAref_Val=https://www.cdc.gov/childrensmentalhealth/data.html

Center on the Developing Child. (2024). *Toxic stress*. https://developingchild.harvard.edu/science/key-concepts/toxic-stress/

Chen, F., & Cui, Y. (2019). Investigating the relation of perceived teacher unfairness to science achievement by hierarchical linear modeling in 52 countries and economies. *Educational Psychology*, *40*(3), 273–295. https://doi.org/10.1080/01443410.2019.1652248

Creswell, J. W., & Poth, C. N., (2018). *Qualitative inquiry and research design:*

Choosing among five approaches (4th ed.). Sage.

Crouch, E., Probst, J. C., Radcliff, E., Bennett, K. J., & McKinney, S. H. (2019). Prevalence of adverse childhood experiences (ACEs) among US children. *Child Abuse & Neglect, 92*, 209–218.

Darling-Hammond, L., Flook, L., Cook-Harvey, C., Barron, B., & Osher, D. (2020). Implications for educational practice of the science of learning and development. *Applied Developmental Science, 24*(2), 97–140.

Dearth-Wesley, T., Herman, A. N., & Whitaker, R. C. (2023). Teacher connection and student perspective-taking and their association with school belonging among adolescents in 62 countries. *International Journal of Adolescence and Youth, 28*(1), Article 2254136. https://doi.org/10.1080/02673843.2023.2254136

Deci, E. L., & Ryan, R. M. (2000). The "what" and "why" of goal pursuits: Human needs and the self-determination of behavior. *Psychological Inquiry, 11*, 227–268.

Faircloth, B. S., & Hamm, J. V. (2005). Sense of belonging among high school students representing 4 ethnic groups. *Journal of Youth and Adolescence, 34*(4), 293–309. https://doi.org/10.1007/s10964-005-5752-7

Fereday, J., & Muir-Cochrane, E. (2006). Demonstrating rigor using thematic analysis: A hybrid approach of inductive and deductive coding and theme development. *International Journal of Qualitative Methods, 5*(1), 80–92.

Fergus, S., & Zimmerman, M. A. (2005). Adolescent resilience: A framework for understanding healthy development in the face of risk. *Annual Review of Public Health, 26*(1), 399–419.

Finkelhor, D. (2020). Trends in adverse childhood experiences (ACEs) in the United States. *Child Abuse & Neglect, 108*, Article 104641. https//doi.org/10.1016/j.chiabu.2020.104641

Frydman, J. S. & Mayor C. (2017). Trauma and early adolescent development: Case examples from a trauma-informed public health middle school program. *Children & Schools, 39*(4). https://doi.org/10.1093/cs/cdx017

García-Moya, I., Bunn, F., Jiménez-Iglesias, A., Paniagua, C., & Brooks, F. M. (2019). The conceptualisation of school and teacher connectedness in adolescent research: A scoping review of literature. *Educational Review, 71*(4), 423–444.

Gini, G., Marino, C., Pozzoli, T., & Holt, M. (2018). Associations between peer victimization, perceived teacher unfairness, and adolescents' adjustment and well-being. *Journal of school psychology, 67*, 56-68.

Goings, R. B., Walker, L. J., & Cotignola-Pickens, H. (2018). School and district leaders' role in diversifying the teacher workforce. *Educational Planning, 25*(3), 7–17.

Goldstein, S., & Brooks, R. B. (2023). The continuing study of resilience in times of a pandemic: This is why we study resilience. In S. Goldstein, & R. B. Brooks (Eds.), *Handbook of Resilience in Children* (3rd ed) (pp. 85–102). Springer.

Goodenow, C., & Grady, K. E. (1993). The relationship of school belonging and friends' values to academic motivation among urban adolescent students. *The Journal of Experimental Education* 62, 60–71. https://doi.org/10.1080/00220973.1993.9943831.

Hellström, L., & Beckman, L. (2021). Life challenges and barriers to help seeking: adolescents' and young adults' voices of mental health. *International Journal of Environmental Research and Public Health*, *18*(24), Article 13101. https://doi.org/10.3390/ijerph182413101

Herman, J. (2015). *Trauma and recovery. The aftermath of violence – from domestic abuse to political terror.* Basic Books.

Jennings, P. (2018). *The trauma-sensitive classroom: Building resilience with compassionate teaching.* W.W. Norton & Company.

Jones, S. M., Bodie, G. D., & Hughes, S. D. (2019). The impact of mindfulness on empathy, active listening, and perceived provisions of emotional support. *Communication Research*, *46*(6), 838–865.

Joos, C. M., McDonald, A., & Wadsworth, M. E. (2019). Extending the toxic stress model into adolescence: Profiles of cortisol reactivity. *Psychoneuroendocrinology, 107*, 46–58. https://doi.org/10.1016/j.psyneuen.2019.05.002

Korpershoek, H., Canrinus, E. T., Fokkens-Bruinsma, M., & De Boer, H. (2020). The relationships between school belonging and students' motivational, social-emotional, behavioural, and academic outcomes in secondary education: A meta-analytic review. *Research Papers in Education*, *35*(6), 641–680.

Maloney, J. E., Whitehead, J., Long, D., Kaufmann, J., Oberle, E., Schonert-Reichl, K. A., Cianfrone, M., Gist, A., & Samji, H. (2024). Supporting adolescent well-being at school: Integrating transformative social and emotional learning and trauma-informed education. *Social and Emotional Learning: Research, Practice, and Policy, 4*, Article 100044. https//doi.org/10.1016/j.sci.2024.100044

Missouri Department of Mental Health and Partners (2019). Missouri model: A developmental framework for trauma-informed approaches. (Rev. ed.) https://dmh.mo.gov/media/pdf/missouri-model-developmental-framework-trauma-informed-approaches

Nardon, L., Hari, A., & Aarma, K. (2021). Reflective interviewing—Increasing social impact through research. *International Journal of Qualitative Methods, 20.* https://doi.org/10.1177/16094069211065233

National Scientific Council on the Developing Child. (2005/2014). Excessive stress disrupts the architecture of the developing brain: Working paper 3. Updated Edition. http://www.developingchild.harvard.edu

Nowell, L. S., Norris, J. M., White, D. E., & Moules, N. J. (2017). Thematic analysis: Striving to meet the trustworthiness criteria. *International Journal of Qualitative Methods, 16*(1). https://doi.org/10.1177/1609406917733847

Proudfoot, K. (2023). Inductive/deductive hybrid thematic analysis in mixed methods research. *Journal of Mixed Methods Research, 17*(3), 308–326. https://doi.

org/10.1177/15586898221126816

Raufelder, D., & Kulakow, S. (2022). The role of social belonging and exclusion at school and the teacher–student relationship for the development of learned helplessness in adolescents. *British Journal of Educational Psychology*, *92*(1), 59–81.

Ruzek, E. A., Hafen, C. A., Allen, J. P., Gregory, A., Mikami, A. Y., & Pianta, R. C. (2016). How teacher emotional support motivates students: The mediating roles of perceived peer relatedness, autonomy support, and competence. *Learning and Instruction*, *42*, 95–103.

Sacks, V., & Murphey, D. (2018). The prevalence of adverse childhood experiences, nationally, by state, and by race or ethnicity. *Child Trends*, *20*, 2018.

Shonkoff, J. P.; Garner, A. S.; Committee on Psychosocial Aspects of Child and Family Health, Committee on Early Childhood, Adoption, and Dependent Care, and Section on Developmental and Behavioral Pediatrics, Siegel, B. S.; Dobbins, M. I.; Earls M. F.; ... & Wood, D. L. (2012). The lifelong effects of early childhood adversity and toxic stress. *Pediatrics*, *129*(1), e232–e246.

Smith, D., Frey N., Pumpian, I., & Fisher, D. (2017). *Building equity: Policies and practices to empower all learners*. ASCD.

Tucker, C., Smith-Adcock, S., & Trepal, H. C. (2011). Relational-cultural theory for middle school counselors. *Professional School Counseling*, *14*(5), 310-316.

VanderWoude, T. R. (2024). *How teacher-student relationships affect child and adolescent resilience.* Theses and Dissertations. 6331. https://scholarsjunction.msstate.edu/td/6331

Venet, A.S. (2021). *Equity-centered trauma-informed education*. W. W. Norton and Company.

Wang, M. T. & Degol, J. (2016). School climate: A review of the construct, measurement, and impact on student outcomes. *Educ Psychol Rev, 28*, 315–352. https://doi.org/10.1007/s10648-015-9319-1

Warren, C. A. (2018). Empathy, teacher dispositions, and preparation for culturally responsive pedagogy. *Journal of Teacher Education, 69*(2), 169–183. https://doi.org/10.1177/0022487117712487

Wentzel, K. R. (2004). Understanding classroom competence: The role of social-motivational and self-processes. In R. V. Kail (Ed.), *Advances in child development and behavior* Vol. 32. (pp. 213–241). Elsevier.

Wickström, A., & Lindholm, S. K. (2020). Young people's perspectives on the symptoms asked for in the Health Behavior in School-Aged Children survey. *Childhood*, *27*(4), 450–467.

Zimmerman, M. A., & Brenner, A. B. (2010). Resilience in adolescence: Overcoming neighborhood disadvantage. In J. W. Reich, A. J. Zautra, & J. S. Hall (Eds.), *Handbook of adult resilience* (pp. 283–308). The Guilford Press.

Zimmerman, M. A., Stoddard, S. A., Eisman, A. B., Caldwell, C. H., Aiyer, S. M., & Miller, A. (2013). Adolescent resilience: Promotive factors that inform prevention. *Child Development Perspectives*, *7*(4), 215–220.

CHAPTER 8

Belonging, Trauma, and Resilience:
Creating a School Environment that Celebrates Human Connection Using a Multisystemic Approach

RENATA SLEDGE

Introduction

ON THE HEELS OF the COVID-19 pandemic, the Surgeon General, Dr. Vivek H. Murthy, raised the alarm about the epidemic of loneliness in America (US Surgeon General, 2023). Loneliness has profound individual and public health implications, as those with meaningful social connections live longer, have fewer physical symptoms of illness, and have lower blood pressure (Uchino, 2006; Uchino et al., 1996). In fact, the absence of social connection has the same risk for premature death as smoking 15 cigarettes a day (US Surgeon General, 2023). Connection and stable relationships early in life profoundly impact development (Bowlby, 1969). Children and adolescents who describe themselves as lonely or depressed have an increased risk of depression and anxiety that lasts up to nine years (Domènech-Abella et al., 2019). Conversely, positive relationships with peers, parents, and teachers are a protective factor against mental illness and improve academic outcomes (DuBois et al., 2011; Steiner et al., 2019).

The burden of social isolation, loneliness, and disconnection is not shared equally across the United States. Black, Indigenous, and People of Color, LGBTQIA+ individuals, those living in low-income neighborhoods, and people who are disabled, unhoused, incarcerated, or unemployed experience systemic barriers to opportunities to reduce isolation. These barriers include hyper-segregated neighborhoods, disinvestment in communal spaces, mass incarceration, and social norms and biases that prevent connection (Wilkerson, 2021). Systemic factors that thwart belonging and social connection compound the adverse effects of trauma and oppression on children (Bernard et al., 2021; Bhargav & Swords, 2022).

Given the ubiquitous nature of school in the lives of children and adolescents, the education system plays a pivotal role in responding to the epidemic of loneliness. Recognizing the intersections between health and school connection, the Centers for Disease Control (2009) identified four factors to promote school connectedness: adult support, positive peer group, commitment to education, and the school environment. This chapter builds on those factors by exploring how belonging, trauma, and resilience connect to students and schools in conjunction with strategies for creating a school environment that celebrates human connection using a multisystemic approach.

Belonging

Synonyms for *belonging* in the research literature include school membership, connectedness, bonding, and relatedness. Goodenow and Grady (1993) defined belonging as "the extent to which students feel personally accepted, respected, included, and supported by others in the school environment" (p. 60). Acknowledging the subjective experience of belonging, Mahar et al. (2013) emphasized that the feeling of value and respect form a reciprocal relationship built on shared values, beliefs, and characteristics. These shared values are mirrored in other definitions, such as the importance of positive emotions (St-Amand et al., 2017). Autonomy is a key feature of many belonging constructs that underline the students' choice to pursue belonging (Hagerty et al., 1992; Mahar et al., 2013).

The Fundamental Need to Belong

Relationships are necessary for individual well-being. Baumeister and Leary (1995) theorize that we have an innate psychological drive to belong to groups through maintaining lasting, positive, and significant interpersonal relationships. Maslow's (1962) hierarchy classifies belonging as a fundamental human need once our basic survival needs are satisfied. Belonging must be satisfied to reach self-actualization. According to social baseline theory (SBT), these relationships are a natural baseline of the brain (Beckes & Coan, 2011). The brain relies on relationships characterized by interdependence, shared goals, and joint attention (Bowlby, 1969; Coan & Sbarra, 2015). Additional laboratory research described by Bernstein et al. (2021) demonstrates that exclusion from relationships negatively impacts affect, mood, self-esteem, and other basic needs. Students who experience relationships characterized by unreliability will assume the need for increased biological resources (e.g., cortisol, oxygen) in the face of threats. Conversely, persons with a history of responsive social support will predict a lower need for biological resources when experiencing a threat (Beckes & Coan, 2011; Coan & Sbarra, 2015).

Belonging in School

The unpredictability, support, and threats to safety and security that students experience influence development from multiple levels. Allen et al.'s (2018) bio-psych-social-ecological model of school belonging (see Figure 8.1) identifies the family as children's first unit of belonging, affirming significant research regarding attachment and trauma (Bowlby, 1969; Bronfenbrenner, 1994; Siegel, 2006). The settings and environment in the bioecological model of development are described in nested structures like Russian dolls using the language of microsystem, mesosystem, exosystem, macrosystem, and chronosystem. The microsystem reflects the activities, social roles, and interpersonal relationships between the developing individual and their context (e.g., the student and the school). The mesosystem explores how two or more settings interact, such as the parents and the teachers. Ecosystems include the interactions between settings that do not directly impact the student. Multisystemic resilience research includes the exosystem as a target for intervention to promote individual student resilience. At the macrosystem and chronosystem levels, students begin to experience communal, historical, and generational trauma.

Figure 8.1
The Bio-Psycho-Socio-Ecological Model (BPSEM) of School Belonging

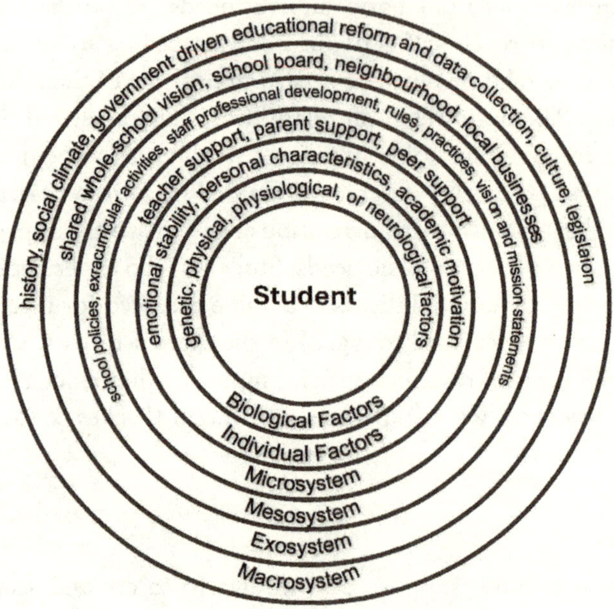

Note: Reprinted by permission from Springer Nature: Springer Nature, Springer eBook, A Multilevel Framework of School Belonging, Kelly-Ann Allen, Margaret L. Kern, 2017.

Trauma

Trauma is often understood from an individual, interpersonal experience in which the student's lack of a sense of safety, agency, dignity, or belonging disrupts their ability to cope with distress (McGlynn-Wright & Briner, 2021). These disruptions to dignity and belonging can include physical violence and the social violence of exclusion. Trauma can also be collective, experienced by kinship, geographical, or historical communities (Davis et al., 2022). When a community is denied access to healing, the trauma becomes historical; when transmitted across generations, trauma is considered intergenerational.

The connection between individual and collective trauma is nuanced (Atallah et al., 2023), and while informed of trauma, mental health, and systems of oppression individually, educators may have limited training on the intersection across these dimensions of well-being (Atallah et al., 2023).

Resilience programs often integrate school belonging into their resilience development programs (Allen et al., 2022). Given the impact of trauma on emotional regulation, attachment, and co-regulation with others, educators and administrators must understand the interacting systems that impact individual, school, and community resilience.

Exclusion and Trauma for Students

The exclusion experienced by marginalized students in their community and schools has biopsychosocial consequences that impact their well-being and relationships (Bernard et al., 2021). For example, the disproportionate levels of suspension, expulsion, or removal from the classroom are literal forms of exclusion that students of color experience from teachers and administrators (Goodkind et al., 2020). Microaggressions, bullying, and the constant vigilance necessary to work with teachers and administrators who have not explored their implicit biases contribute to an environment of toxic stress for students. This extended exposure to toxic stress impacts development and cognitive functions (e.g., attention, memory, language, and emotional and behavioral regulation) in children and adolescents because prolonged exposure results in high levels of stress hormones, such as cortisol (Hamoudi et al., 2015). Learning can be inhibited when these cognitive functions are negatively impacted (Shi & Qu, 2021).

Trauma-Sensitive Programs in Schools

Attention to belonging and relationships in trauma-sensitive programs is validated by the academic and psychosocial benefits students demonstrate when they feel they belong in school. Academic benefits associated with belonging include improved grades, self-efficacy, higher academic motivation, less absenteeism, less truancy, and more positive attitudes toward learning (Allen et al., 2018). Psychosocial benefits of a sense of belonging include increased perceived positive self-esteem, self-efficacy, life satisfaction, happiness, friendship, and optimism (Allen & Bowles, 2012). The connection to belonging is further amplified by the role belonging plays as a protective factor against psychopathology and stress.

Evidence-based programs to promote resilience and trauma sensitivity in schools train educators to support healing within the school context. However, these programs are often administered in historically white institutions that focus on the after-effects of individual and collective trauma rather than on dismantling systems that sustain harm (Atallah et al., 2021). Davis et al. (2022) highlight the impact of schools in disrupting systemic trauma perpetuated by schools with programming that promotes systemic resilience. Educators, administrators, and communities should develop intersectional and multisystemic programs with a nuanced understanding of resilience responsive to students' individual and collective trauma contexts.

Resilience

Existing school resilience programs reference the ecological theory of development (Bronfenbrenner, 1994) to highlight the importance of integrating parents and other community systems in socio-emotional learning programs (Fein et al., 2021; Goodkind et al., 2020; Greenwood & Kelly, 2019; Greig et al., 2021; Masten, 2021; Saleem et al., 2022; Zinn et al., 2020). Atallah et al. (2023) document that many trauma-sensitive programs with resilience outcomes have interventions designed to create inclusive environments where all students and staff feel safe and supported. However, these programs do not implicitly, nor explicitly, acknowledge the impact and influence of systemic oppression in perpetuating harm to minoritized students and educators. Resilience theory has further adapted Bronfenbrenner's (1994) systemic understanding from individual systems that bounce back to a multisystemic transformation that increases the capacity of individuals, organizations, and communities to encourage change on a systemic level (Ungar, 2021). Understanding the development of resilience theory from the first wave of bouncing back from adversity towards a multisystemic approach that centers the margins is necessary to develop programs in schools that create opportunities for healing and justice with equitable access to culturally relevant resources (Ungar, 2021; Atallah et al., 2021)

Bounce Back

Early research on resilience was inspired by evidence that children exposed to traumatic events had disparate outcomes. The first wave of resilience research in psychology, human development, and psychiatry attributed the ability of individuals to bounce back from adversity to personal traits of resilience (Walsh, 2002). As Atallah et al. (2021) described, frontline helping professions began challenging the interplay of vulnerability and protective factors by challenging research to consider the context of adversity. Resilience began to be operationalized beyond the characteristics of positivity, optimism, and strengths, including the family and social setting of the individual.

Bounce Forward

The emerging systems orientation of resilience research established a *bounce forward* approach that considered resilience a relational, intergenerational, and ecosystemic process. This second wave of resilience theories did not consider mental health problems (i.e., post-traumatic stress disorder) and growth as mutually exclusive. Instead, resilience was increasingly understood as the intersection between victimization and agency (Ungar, 2010; Walsh, 2016). Simultaneous with the increased growth mindset of this third wave, an effort to operationalize and measure resilience to evaluate best-practice programs shifted the understanding of resilience as a process to an outcome. Western dominant values of positive attributes such as high self-esteem, educational achievement, and prosocial behaviors measured resilience outcomes (Goodkind et al., 2020).

Centering the Margins and Multisystemic Resilience

By centering the Western dominant values on resilience, researchers and practitioners perpetuated the marginalization of minority students by ignoring the historical and social intersections that facilitate interpersonal, collective, and historical trauma. To center the margins (Atallah et al., 2021), the third wave of resilience research shifts to understanding the intersecting racial, gender, and class structures that impact well-being (see Figure 8.2). The resulting transdisciplinary focus recognizes that individual resilience is facilitated by resilience in families, schools, communities, cultures, and religions (Masten, 2021; Ungar, 2021). The multisystemic resilience perspective deepens Bronfenbrenner's (1994) ecological theory of development from understanding the way context informs development to understanding how the various levels (e.g., microsystems, mesosystems, exosystems, chronosystems) influence the individual response to stress and trauma

Figure 8.2
Three Waves of Resilience Research

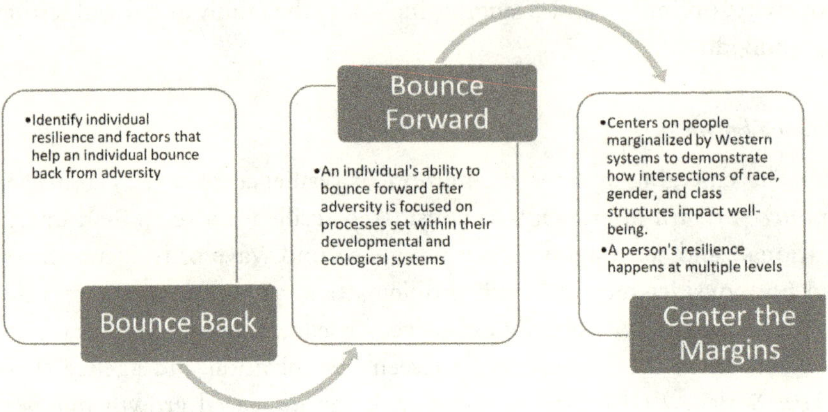

Note: Three waves of resilience research as described by Walsh (2016), Atallah et al., (2021), and Ungar (2021).

Organizational Improvement: Belonging and Resilience in Action

A multisystemic and multifactorial response is required to address the epidemic of loneliness in America, generally, and our schools, specifically (Allen et al., 2022). The Surgeon General's advisory report identified a six-pillar approach to advance social connection (2023). These include:

1. Strengthen social infrastructure and local communities;
2. Enact pro-connection public policies;
3. Mobilize the health sector;
4. Reform digital environments;
5. Deepen our knowledge; and
6. Build a culture of connection.

The education system can address pillars 1, 2, 5, and 6 with continued attention to resilience and belonging through attention to relationships in school-based trauma response programs. Cole et al. (2013) describe trauma-sensitive schools as places "in which all students feel safe, welcomed, and supported and where addressing trauma's impact on learning on a schoolwide basis is at the center of its educational mission" (p. 11). Further, Harris and Fallot's (2001) change process centers on relationships and multisystemic philosophy in their key concepts that include safety, trustworthiness, choice, collaboration, and empowerment.

The Centers for Disease Control (2009) seemed to anticipate the Surgeon General's recommendations by identifying six strategies to promote school connectedness. These strategies are still recognized as meaningful steps to promote belonging (Allen et al., 2018) and are discussed in the following paragraphs.

1. ***Create decision-making processes that facilitate student, family, and community engagement, academic achievement, and staff empowerment.***

   As Kotter (1995) describes, an empowered coalition with a shared vision is integral to the change process. While leadership is essential in facilitating trauma-informed schools, empowerment is vital to resilience (Cole et al., 2013; Goodkind et al., 2020; Imad, 2022). Engaging students, educators, and community partners in strategic planning shifts the focus from resilient students to resilient communities (Masten, 2021).

2. ***Provide education and opportunities for families to be actively involved in their children's academic and school lives.***

   Families, like schools that collaborate as a functional unit with key resilience-promoting processes such as open emotional expression that facilitates shared decision-making mitigate the risk of maladaptation from a crisis, thereby promoting family resilience (Masten, 2021; Walsh, 2003, 2016). Partnering with community organizations to reduce barriers and capitalize on family strengths in the community can help foster high family expectations for academic performance (Allen & Bowles, 2012). These strategies include a range of interventions, including providing tangible resources such as transportation and parent workshops about positive communication skills and prioritizing educational goals.

3. ***Provide students with academic, emotional, and social skills necessary to actively engage in school.***

   Academic readiness is a multidimensional construct that includes social, emotional, and cognitive areas. The coalition committed to creating a community of belonging should consider a range of activities to ensure students have the skills to engage, including tutoring, socio-emotional learning programs, and strategies to promote autonomy. Students who have experienced interpersonal or collective trauma are more likely to experience impaired emotional regulation and would benefit from strengths-based programs such as positive competitions and future planning (Allen et al., 2022).

4. ***Use effective classroom management and teaching methods to foster a positive learning environment.***

   The contextual support features of structure, autonomy support, and relatedness provide an outline for facilitating relationship development that provides a safe school environment for students and educators, facilitating growth and autonomy (Deci & Ryan, 2000; Robb, 2000). Structure is provided in environments that communicate clear expectations and consequences, provide optimal challenges, and provide positive feedback regarding competence. Autonomy support encourages freedom of expression by facilitating choices and decision-making. Relatedness, a sense of connectedness and belonging, allows students to organize their self-perception as worthy and their social world as trustworthy. Classroom empowerment intervention facilitates structural and systemic change and can promote critical consciousness for marginalized students, deepening their own sense of identity (Atallah et al., 2023; Goodkind et al., 2020). This requires schools to reconsider behavior management in more restorative terms, shifting from discipline to relational accountability (Atallah et al., 2021, 2023).

5. ***Provide professional development and support for teachers and other school staff to enable them to meet the diverse cognitive, emotional, and social needs of children and adolescents.***

   Educators come to school with their own complicated stories, complicated by their personal experiences with interpersonal and collective trauma. Community coalitions should work with schools to hire educators who have the cognitive and practical knowledge necessary to function in trauma-informed environments (Allen & Bowles, 2012). However, the responsibility continues beyond the offer letter; educators must also feel a sense of belonging to the school and community (Greenwood & Kelly, 2019). Community leaders and administrators should develop policies and practices that support staff well-being, garner community support for educators, and provide continuing education to develop competence and confidence in addressing the social needs of students.

6. ***Create trusting and caring relationships that promote open communication among administrators, teachers, staff, students, families, and communities.***

   Just as these recommendations begin with creating an empowered coalition to institutionalize the change of a trauma-informed approach that embraces belonging, stakeholders should be engaged in an ongoing manner in evaluating and adapting policies and practices (Kotter, 1995). Resilience is the response to adversity, explicitly and implicitly suggesting change. Creating environments with multiple feedback processes, with a mutual focus on human connection, can help the dynamic school system adapt to the challenges that threaten the students' function, survival, and development (Cefai, 2021; Masten, 2021).

Conclusion

This chapter underscores the critical relationship among belonging, trauma, resilience, and the profound impact they collectively exert on the educational experiences of children and adolescents. As we continue to navigate the aftermath of the COVID-19 pandemic, the Surgeon General's acknowledgment of the loneliness epidemic in America is a stark reminder of the importance of belonging for individual and public health. The disparities in experiences of social isolation and exclusion are intricately linked to systemic barriers faced by marginalized communities. To promote belonging and student resilience, schools should target interventions and programs that address the micro-, meso-, exo-, and macro-systems in which students are situated. The school community plays a pivotal role in belonging, resilience, and healing for developing children. The Surgeon General and the CDC guidelines provide a roadmap for creating trauma-informed and inclusive school environments that foster positive relationships and contribute to the overall well-being of students, educators, and communities. School systems can create coalitions that empower all stakeholders to engage in decision-making processes while encouraging families to prioritize educational goals. School programs can promote student strengths and ensure educators are confident in restorative classroom practices to address students' social, behavioral, and educational needs. Finally, school systems should use multiple feedback processes to evaluate nimble systems that respond to the changing needs of students and communities. Ultimately, human connection is at the forefront of educational practices, with an intrinsic value in promoting resilience, reducing trauma impacts, and nurturing individuals' holistic development within a larger societal context.

References

Allen, K. A., & Bowles, T. (2012). Belonging as a guiding principle in the education of adolescents. *Australian Journal of Educational and Developmental Psychology*, *12*, 108–119.

Allen, K. A., Jamshidi, N., Berger, E., Reupert, A., Wurf, G., & May, F. (2022). Impact of school-based interventions for building school belonging in adolescence: A systematic review. *Educational Psychology Review*, *34*(1), 229–257. https://doi.org/10.1007/s10648-021-09621-w

Allen, K., Kern, M. L., Vella-Brodrick, D., Hattie, J., & Waters, L. (2018). What schools need to know about fostering school belonging: A meta-analysis. *Educational Psychology Review*, *30*(1), 1–34. https://doi.org/10.1007/s10648-016-9389-8

Atallah, D. G., Bacigalupe, G., & Repetto, P. (2021). Centering at the margins: Critical community resilience praxis. *Journal of Humanistic Psychology*, *61*(6), 875–905. https://doi.org/10.1177/0022167818825305

Atallah, D. G., Koslouski, J. B., Perkins, K. N., Marscio, C., Robinson, R. L., Del Rio, M. G., & Porche, M. V. (2023). The trauma and learning policy initiative (TLPI)'s inquiry-based process: Mapping systems change toward resilience. *Journal of Community Psychology*, *51*(7), 2943–2963. https://doi.org/10.1002/jcop.23067

Baumeister, R. F., & Leary, M. R. (1995). The need to belong: Desire for interpersonal attachments as a fundamental human motivation. *Interpersonal Development*, *117*(3), 57–89. https://doi.org/10.4324/9781351153683-3

Beckes, L., & Coan, J. (2011). Social Baseline Theory: The role of social proximity in emotion and economy of action. *Social and Personality Psychology Compass, (12)*, 976–988. https://doi.org/10.1111/j.1751-9004.2011.00400.x

Bernard, D. L., Calhoun, C. D., Banks, D. E., Halliday, C. A., Hughes-Halbert, C., & Danielson, C. K. (2021). Making the "C-ACE" for a culturally-informed adverse childhood experiences framework to understand the pervasive mental health impact of racism on Black youth. *Journal of Child & Adolescent Trauma, 14*, 233–247. https://doi.org/10.1007/s40653-020-00319-9

Bernstein, M. J., Neubauer, A. B., Benfield, J. A., Potter, L., & Smyth, J. M. (2021). Within-person effects of inclusion and exclusion on well-being in daily life. *Personal Relationships, 28*(4), 940–960. https://doi.org/10.1111/pere.12399

Bhargav, M., & Swords, L. (2022). Role of thwarted belongingness, perceived burdensomeness and psychological distress in the association between adverse childhood experiences and suicidal ideation in college students. *BJ Psych Open, 8*(e39), 1–7. https://doi.org/10.1192/bjo.2021.1087

Bowlby, J. (1969). *Attachment: Attachment and loss volume one.* Hogarth.

Brody, G. H., Yu, T., Miller, G. E., & Chen, E. (2016). Resilience in adolescence, health, and psychosocial outcomes. *Pediatrics, 138*(6). https://doi.org/10.1542/peds.2016-1042

Bronfenbrenner, U. (1994). Ecological models of human development. In *International Encyclopedia of Education* (pp. 287–290). Oxford. https://doi.org/10.4324/9780203730386-13

Cefai, C. (2021). A transactional, whole-school approach to resilience. In M Ungar (Ed.), *Multisystemic Resilience.* Oxford University Press.

Centers for Disease Control. (2009). *School connectedness; strategies for increasing-protective factors among youth.* https://stacks.cdc.gov/view/cdc/5767

Coan, J. A., & Sbarra, D. A. (2015). Social baseline theory: The social regulation of risk and effort. *Current Opinion in Psychology, 1*, 87. https://doi.org/10.1016/J.COPSYC.2014.12.021

Cole, S., Eisner, A., Gregory, M., & Ristuccia, J. (2013). *Helping traumatized children learn: Creating and advocating for trauma-sensitive schools (Vol 2).* Publisher.

Davis, W., Petrovic, L., Whalen, K., Danna, L., Zeigler, K., Brewton, A., Joseph, M., Baker, C. N., & Overstreet, S. (2022). Centering trauma-informed approaches in schools within a social justice framework. *Psychology in the Schools, 59*(12), 2453–2470. https://doi.org/10.1002/pits.22664

Deci, E. L., & Ryan, R. M. (2000). The "what" and "why" of goal pursuits: human needs and the self-determination of behavior. *Psychological Inquiry, 11*, 227–268. https://doi.org/10.1207/S15327965PLI1104_01

Domènech-Abella, J., Mundó, J., Haro, J. M., & Rubio-Valera, M. (2019). Anxiety, depression, loneliness and social network in the elderly: Longitudinal associations from The Irish Longitudinal Study on Ageing (TILDA). *Journal of Affective Disorders, 246*, 82–88.

DuBois, D., Portillo, N., Rhodes, J., Silverthorn, N., & Valentine, J. (2011). How effective are mentoring programs for youth? a systematic assessment of the evidence. *Psychological Science in the Public Interest*, *12*(2), 57–91.

Fein, E. H., Kataoka, S., Aralis, H., Lester, P., Marlotte, L., Morgan, R., & Ijadi-Maghsoodi, R. (2021). Implementing a school-based, trauma-informed resilience curriculum for parents. *Social Work in Public Health*, *36*(7–8), 795–805. https://doi.org/10.1080/19371918.2021.1958116

Goodenow, C., & Grady, K. (1993). The relationship of school belonging and friends' values to academic motivation among urban adolescent students. *The Journal of Experimental Education*, *62*(1), 60–81. https://www.jstor.org/stable/20152398

Goodkind, S., Brinkman, B. G., & Elliott, K. (2020). Redefining resilience and reframing resistance: Empowerment programming with Black girls to address societal inequities. *Behavioral Medicine*, *46*(3–4), 317–329. https://doi.org/10.1080/08964289.2020.1748864

Greenwood, L., & Kelly, C. (2019). A systematic literature review to explore how staff in schools describe how a sense of belonging is created for their pupils. *Emotional and Behavioural Difficulties*, *24*(1), 3–19. https://doi.org/10.1080/13632752.2018.1511113

Greig, J., Bailey, B., Abbott, L., & Brunzell, T. (2021). Trauma-informed integral leadership: leading school communities with a systems-aware approach. *International Journal of Whole Schooling*, *17*(1), 62–97.

Hagerty, B. M. K., Lynch-Sauer, J., Patusky, K. L., Bouwsema, M., & Collier, P. (1992). Sense of belonging: A vital mental health concept. *Archives of Psychiatric Nursing, VI*(3), *172–177.*

Hamoudi, A., Murray, D. W., Sorensen, L., & Fontaine, A. (2015). *Self-Regulation and Toxic Stress: A Review of Ecological, Biological, and Developmental Studies of Self-Regulation and Stress.* http://www.acf.hhs.gov/programs/opre/resource/self-regulation-and-toxic-stress-a-review-of-ecological-biological-and-developmental-studies-of-self-regulation-and-stress

Harris, M., & Fallot, R. (Eds.). (2001). *Using trauma theory to design service systems: New directions for mental health services.* Jossey-Bass.

Imad, M. (2022). Trauma-informed education for wholeness: Strategies for faculty & advisors. *New Directions for Student Services*, *2022*(177), 39–47. https://doi.org/10.1002/ss.20413

Kotter, J. (1995, May–June). Leading change: Why transformation efforts fail. *Harvard Business Review.*

Mahar, A. L., Cobigo, V., & Stuart, H. (2013). Conceptualizing belonging. *Disability and Rehabilitation*, *35*(12), 1026–1032. https://doi.org/10.3109/09638288.2012.717584

Maslow, A. (1962). *Towards a psychology of need.* Van Nostrand.

Masten, A. (2021). Resilience in developmental systems. In Michael Ungar (Ed.), *Mutlisystemic Resilience.* Oxford University Press.

McGlynn-Wright, T., & Briner, L. (2021). *Integrative Trauma and Healing Framework.*

Robb, S. (2000). The effect of therapeutic music interventions on the behavior of hospitalized children in isolation: Developing a contextual support model of music therapy. *Journal of Music Therapy*, *37*(2), 118–146. https://doi.org/https://doi.org/10.1093/jmt/37.2.118

Saleem, F. T., Howard, T. C., & Langley, A. K. (2022). Understanding and addressing racial stress and trauma in schools: A pathway toward resistance and healing. *Psychology in the Schools*, *59*(12), 2506–2521. https://psycnet.apa.org/doi/10.1002/pits.22615

Shi, Y. Q. & Qu S. W. (2021). Cognition and academic performance: Mediating role of personality characteristics and psychology health. *Frontiers in Psychology,* 12, Article 774548. https://doi.org/10.3389/fpsyg.2021.774548

Siegel, D. (2006). An interpersonal neurobiology approach to psychotherapy: Awareness, mirror neurons, and neural plasticity in the development of well-being. *Psychiatric Annals*, *36*(4), 248-256.

St-Amand, J., Girard, S., & Smith, J. (2017). Sense of belonging at school: Defining attributes, determinants, and sustaining strategies. *IAFOR Journal of Education*, *5*(2), 105–120. https://doi.org/10.22492/ije.5.2.05

Steiner, R., Sheremenko, G., Lesesne, C., Dittus, P., Sieving, R., & Ethier, K. (2019). Adolescent connectedness and adult health outcomes. *Pediatrics*, *144*(1) , Article e20183766.

US Surgeon General. (2023). *Our Epidemic of Loneliness and Isolation.* https://www.hhs.gov/sites/default/files/surgeon-general-social-connection-advisory.pdf

Uchino, B. N. (2006). Social Support and health: A review of physiological processes potentially underlying links to disease outcomes. *Journal of Behavioral Medicine*, *29*(4). https://doi.org/10.1007/s10865-006-9056-5

Uchino, B. N., Cacioppo, J. T., & Kiecolt-Glaser, J. K. (1996). The relationship between social support and physiological processes: A review with emphasis on underlying mechanisms and implications for health. *Psychological Bulletin*, *119*(3), 488–531. https://doi.org/10.1037/0033-2909.119.3.488

Ungar, M. (2010). Families as navigators and negotiators: facilitating culturally and contextually specific expressions of resilience. *Family Process, 49*(3), 421–436.

Ungar, M. (2021). Modeling multisystemic resilience. In Michael Ungar (Ed.), *Multisystemic Resilience.* Oxford University Press.

Walsh, F. (2002). A family resilience framework: Innovative practice applications. *Family Relations*, *51*(2), 130. https://doi.org/10.1111/j.1741-3729.2002.00130.x

Walsh, F. (2003). Family resilience: a framework for clinical practice. *Family Process*, *42*(1), 1–18. https://doi.org/10.1111/j.1545-5300.2003.00001.x

Walsh, F. (2016). Family resilience: a developmental systems framework. *European Journal of Developmental Psychology*, *13*(3), 313–324. https://doi.org/10.10

80/17405629.2016.1154035

Wilkerson, R. (2021). *Socially Connected Communities. Solutions for Social Isolation.* Healthy Places by Design

Zinn, M. E., Huntley, E. D., & Keating, D. P. (2020). Resilience in adolescence: Prospective self moderates the association of early life adversity with externalizing problems. Journal of Adolescence, *81*, 61-72.

CHAPTER 9

The Realities of Trauma-Informed Practices: Teachers' Perspectives

Katherina Roeder

Michael's Story

Years ago, I stepped through the doors of a therapeutic school, not realizing then the profound journey it would ignite: a journey of empathy, resilience, and boundless learning. I discovered that my new reality as an educator would mean working intensely with students from first grade through high school age whose lived experiences included severe cases of neglect and physical, psychological, and sexual abuse. Each of these children had a traumatic background, and, as one of their teachers, I worked daily toward changing the trajectory of their futures.

A therapeutic school is a school that addresses social, emotional, and behavioral concerns. Students who attend these schools cannot attend typical public or private school settings because of potentially volatile behaviors. For example, some students have an explosive disorder, which causes them to act violently for no reason that is discernible to a layperson.

One of these students was Michael. Michael's life had been profoundly shaped by generational trauma. His grandmother's involvement in drug-related crimes led to her imprisonment, establishing a bleak family precedent. Michael's mother followed a similar path, becoming incarcerated while carrying him in her womb. Throughout his upbringing, his mother's repeated incarcerations resulted in Michael's neglect and eventual placement in foster care. As a child, Michael exhibited many destructive behaviors. He frequently hit and kicked other students, screamed, yelled, and was generally disruptive. He struggled with following directions and would try to attack other students. Teachers and social workers had to employ multiple physical restraints, which caused the teachers themselves to experience secondary traumatic stress.

Teachers worked diligently to change the trajectory of his path, employing various strategies and interventions to support his development and well-being. One of the things that helped Michael was the consistency of care teachers and others used to help him. Even with these supports, however, his continued poor choices, including vandalism and possession of narcotics, led to encounters with the law. A stint in juvenile detention brought him face to face with remorse, leading to a newfound interest in improving his life.

The Investment: Trauma-Informed Practices

To support him, Michael's teachers and counselors made concerted efforts to guide him toward a different future. Using trauma-informed practices to address his trauma-based life experiences, teachers and counselors created a safe and supportive classroom environment. This included consistent routines and clear expectations to reduce anxiety and foster a sense of security. School personnel worked to form trusting relationships based on understanding and respect to provide Michael with a pathway to emotional stability.

The school offered emotional and behavioral support through counseling and social work, focusing on guidance and positive decision-making. Instead of punitive measures, restorative practices encouraged accountability and personal growth, helping Michael reflect on his actions. Additionally, a trauma-sensitive curriculum incorporating mindfulness and social-emotional learning activities supported his emotional regulation and sense of belonging.

Michael graduated high school with passing grades and eventually joined the military. He later contacted school staff, expressing gratitude for steering him in the right direction. He was thankful for the support and guidance that helped him turn his life around.

Michael's story demonstrates the need for a culture of trauma-informed care (Fallot & Harris, 2011; Harris & Fallot, 2001) and shows how these approaches can significantly impact students facing similar challenges by fostering resilience and promoting positive change.

The Cost: Secondary Traumatic Stress

As rewarding as it is to know that students like Michael can eventually succeed, the toll it took on me was much more significant than I realized. In fact, due to the secondary traumatic stress and anxiety it created, I eventually left this school for what I hoped would be a calmer environment. At least I stayed in teaching. In a 2022 report, the National Education Association reported that nearly 55% of the teachers polled said they expected to leave the profession earlier than planned due to burnout (Jotkoff, 2022). Part of the reason for such a high rate of burnout is due to teachers always being on high alert and always having to be prepared for a traumatic event, which can cause secondary traumatic stress (Heffernan et al., 2022). With so many students experiencing adverse events, teachers are constantly exposed to those students' traumatic stories, causing teachers to suffer from secondary traumatic stress. "Educators often find themselves having to take on the role of counselors, supporting the emotional healing of their students, not just their academic growth," (Lander, 2018, para. 1).

Students who experience trauma are not the exception. They are among the 66% of children who, by the age of 16, have been exposed to some form of childhood trauma (Substance Abuse Mental Health Services Administration [SAMSHA], 2021, para. 1). This includes witnessing or being victims of domestic violence, sexual assault, community or school violence, physical or sexual abuse, natural disasters, military deployment or loss of a parent, and loss of a close family member in a violent manner (SAMHSA, 2021). For our students, trauma is often too close to home. According to the World Health Organization (WHO), nearly 400 million children are exposed to physical or psychological violence from caregivers or parents (WHO, 2024, para 1). When the world shut down in 2020, COVID-19 pandemic-related isolation policies complicated students' trauma and toxic stress even more, causing some young people to experience additional socioeconomic issues, illness, death, and domestic abuse (Bridgland et al., 2021).

Often, the experience of trauma affects how individuals approach relationships, making them reluctant to engage in available social services. In educational settings, this may manifest as students displaying heightened anxiety, withdrawal, or distrust towards teachers and peers, potentially deterring their academic performance and social integration. Additionally, students who experience trauma may have difficulty concentrating in class and experience emotional dysregulation, manifesting in negative behaviors in the classroom, impacting classroom dynamics and inhibiting student learning (Bridgland et al., 2021). These behaviors can create challenges for educators in fostering a supportive and inclusive learning environment, necessitating the implementation of trauma-informed practices to effectively address and alleviate the impact of trauma on students' educational experiences.

Creating Cultures of Trauma-Informed Care

In 2001, Roger Fallot and Maxine Harris promoted using trauma theory to design mental health service systems. Their basis for creating a trauma-informed system included four basic principles: understanding trauma, understanding the consumer survivor, understanding services, and understanding the service relationship (Harris & Fallot, 2001). They noted:

> Systems service individuals without even being aware of the trauma that occurred. This lack of awareness can result in failure to make appropriate referrals for trauma services. It can also result in inadvertent re-traumatization when a service system's usual operating procedures trigger a reemergence or an exacerbation of trauma symptoms. (p. 3)

Schools are, in essence, service systems that provide services (education) to stakeholders (students). Fallot and Harris have based the systems theory on five core values: safety, trustworthiness, choice, collaboration, and empowerment, to address the needed organizational change. Their goal has been to create trauma-informed cultures that permeate every aspect of an organization, including schools, teachers, administrators, policymakers, and stakeholders (Fallot & Harris, 2011; Harris & Fallot, 2001). Putting theory into practice, they have outlined a series of steps that help guide policymakers. Their process includes several steps that encompass initial planning (Fallot & Harris, 2011):

Table 9.1
Trauma-Informed Action Steps

Step	Action Involved
Initial planning	• establish administrative support • form trauma initiative workgroups; gather representation from stakeholders • create awareness • identify trauma-awareness champions

Kickoff training event	• include staff presentations on
	  • trauma-informed cultures
	  • relevance of trauma on the work of the agency or institution
	  • detailed discussions to motivate the change process

Short-term follow-up	• apply ideas from the training
	• create and use a self-assessment planning protocol
	• plan is developed and reviewed by administration and other stakeholders
	• conduct educational events on trauma
	• garner community-based consultants who
	  • provide feedback
	  • address barriers
	  • assist in strategy development

Long-term follow-up: revisit the program after six to nine months	• review progress
	• discuss sustainability
	  • incorporate trauma-informed questions into satisfaction surveys
	  • build consultation in school practices
	  • add implementation plans to the quality assurance process

Ultimately, this long-term protocol seeks to build lasting organizational change by injecting trauma-informed values, such as those found in the Missouri Model for Trauma-Informed Schools (2019), into the organizational culture. Making these changes requires long-term commitment and often requires outside stakeholders, such as members of state mental health agencies and education departments.

While school districts across the United States have started incorporating trauma-informed training, this process takes significant time and is an intensive process (Huang et al., 2014). Several steps are required to create a true trauma-informed environment that includes targeted support, including training on self-regulation and emotional and behavioral skill-building

(Missouri Model for Trauma-Informed Schools, 2019). Providing a comprehensive framework encompassing understanding, procedures, and principles, this model equips schools with the necessary tools to create supportive environments where students can thrive despite their experiences. Its emphasis on collaboration and the incorporation of its five key principles underscores the importance of holistic approaches to trauma-informed practice. Moreover, the model's systematic approach to implementation, from pre-trauma awareness to trauma-informed stages, demonstrates a thoughtful and effective strategy for promoting lasting change in education settings. (See more about the Missouri Model in Chapter 1.)

Roadblocks and Barriers to Implementing Trauma-Informed Practices

Despite the best professional development, teachers often hit perceived and practical roadblocks and barriers that prevent the implementation of trauma-informed practices (Grant & Hill, 2020; Sharkey et al., 2024). Some perceived barriers include lack of leadership and school support (Duong et al., 2020), lack of time to implement trauma-informed content due to academic timelines, increased emotional and behavioral student outbursts, and the inability for teacher self-regulation (Owens et al., 2023).

In a 2022 study, I asked 99 teachers to share their experiences implementing trauma-informed practices. It became clear that despite the research supporting the need for trauma-informed practices and the assumed support to implement them, teachers reported barriers that impede them from doing so consistently (Roeder, 2022). These barriers highlight the reality of the daily work involved in implementing trauma-informed educational practices. The perceived challenges regarding implementing trauma-informed practices included a lack of consistent support from the administration, a lack of additional personnel to aid in implementing trauma-informed practices, a lack of positive school culture, and a lack of communication between educators and administrators.

Teacher Perceived Barrier: Lack of Support from Administrators

Among those teachers who had participated in the 2022 study and had gone to training, there were numerous reports that, while they attempted to implement the trauma-informed practices they had been taught, they sometimes received mixed messages from their administrators. Sara (pseudonym), an ELA teacher, said, "There is negative criticism from administrators for allowing students time to regulate rather than be on learning tasks." Jenny, another teacher, lamented, "Administrators expect teachers to continue teaching despite the need to attend to students' trauma-induced behaviors." Other teachers noted that they felt that principals use the ideas of trauma-informed practices as "a reason for not giving consequences."

Teachers' perceptions of administrators' lack of support could be tied to not being aware of what support their schools offer. When asked what supports were available to them to implement trauma-informed practices, several teachers responded with phrases such as: "none that I'm aware of," "unsure," "unknown," "none," and "no idea" (Roeder, 2022). This lack of knowledge about the support that existed in their schools speaks to a lack of a trauma-informed culture necessary to truly be trauma-informed. According to the Missouri Model, one indicator that a school is truly trauma-informed is that "All aspects of the organization have been reviewed and revised to reflect a trauma-informed approach" (The Missouri Model, 2019 p. 12) and "The organization and staff become advocates and champions of trauma-informed cultures within their community" (p. 13). If teachers are not aware of the support their schools have to offer, and if they feel their administrators are not supportive, then these schools are not immersed in a trauma-informed culture as described by the Missouri Model.

Teacher Perceived Barrier: Underprepared

Despite having received trauma-informed training, the teachers I surveyed felt underprepared to help their students who were experiencing mental health crises (Roeder, 2022). Participants commented that they felt like they were on their own and that there was no time for other needed training. Other comments illustrated teachers' frustration with a lack of preparation and ability to practice what they had learned. "There is not enough time or space to do it," commented Janie, a secondary teacher. "There is not enough time when there are 24 kids in my class," said Sam, an elementary teacher. These situations can lead to teacher burnout as teachers lament the lack of support from parents and administrators. They said they felt they were catering to students rather than teaching them.

Other teachers felt they were in over their heads and that the training had left them somewhat exposed. "Trauma-informed training is not enough for teachers," explained Sandy, a reading teacher. She went on to explain that the trauma their students experienced left them feeling helpless as they were not able to provide proper mental health support. "We are not trained psychiatrists or counselors," cautioned secondary math teacher Michelle.

Teachers who participated in interviews were concerned that schools were expecting too much out of them. One teacher stated:

> My concern is that the system is now expecting teachers to wear yet another hat at a professional level that most are not trained to handle properly—a professional development training or a video pale in comparison to a degree in social work, psychology and mental health counseling.

Even though many school districts employ school counselors and use social services or social worker resources, many have caseloads that far exceed their ability to attend to all the students' needs properly. In fact, according to a 2024 National Association of School Psychologists (NASP) report, there was just one psychologist for every 1,065 K–12 students in the United States during the 2034-2024 school year (National Association of School Psychologists [NASP], 2024, para. 1). The NASP recommends a ratio of 500 students per school psychologist (NASP, 2024). Simply put, there is a shortage of school psychologists in the US.

Teacher Perceived Barrier: Conflicting Priorities

Given the immense academic curriculum teachers are charged with covering each year, trauma-informed practices can take time away from instruction. If administrators are not supportive, teachers cannot implement such practices with fidelity. One of my study participants explained it this way:

> I think the pressure on teachers to cover material, assess, collect data, document, everything is overwhelming enough and then add in a couple of students having a meltdown—It's easy to just label kids as behavior problems and try to get them out of the room rather than work through the issues. This is why we need more counselors and social workers. One teacher cannot process trauma and keep 20+ other kids engaged and on target in curriculum.

Teachers are finding themselves having to choose between helping students through mental health crises and instruction or planning for instruction. Christa, a math teacher who participated in my study, wrote, "There are many times when things don't go according to my plans because of the implementation of trauma-informed practices. I often lose my plan time to be with students." In a meta-analysis on secondary traumatic stress and compassion fatigue, Ormiston et al. (2022) noted that stress from attempting to manage limited time against increased workloads leads to compassion fatigue.

The National Education Association reports that when teachers must take instructional time to "address disruptive behavior, teaching and learning for the entire class can suffer" (NEA, 2024, para. 5). While the teachers who participated in this study expressed frustration about having to split their attention between instruction and attending to students' mental health needs, a literature review revealed a scarcity of studies on this topic. Researchers are simply not exploring the impact of adding this task to teachers' roles. Most studies are focused on best practices for implementing trauma-informed care in schools, which speaks to the continued culture of adding to teachers' responsibilities without providing additional resources.

Teacher Perceived Barrier: Secondary Traumatic Stress

Teachers also reported that secondary traumatic stress was becoming more prevalent and becoming a burden in their daily work. Cassie, a social studies teacher, responded to the survey by writing, "We do have secondary trauma. The more you seek to understand your students, learn about them, and want to help them, it can wear on you emotionally." One consequence of Secondary Trauma Stress (STS) is that teachers tend to experience burnout or compassion fatigue and leave the profession early in their careers (Walker, 2019).

Trauma-informed specialist Laura McGuire (2024) coined the term *empty cup syndrome* to refer to situations where so many teachers experience being emotionally empty themselves, but they are still expected to work with trauma-impacted students with compassion and empathy. Additionally, if teachers are burned out, they are sometimes shamed for it (McGuire, 2024). Too often, if teachers seem disengaged or overwhelmed, they are perceived as not doing their jobs adequately.

How School Administrators Can Help

It is vital that school administrators recognize when teachers are at risk of experiencing secondary traumatic stress, and it is vital that they respond accordingly. School districts need to have polices established so teachers know their options. Teachers need to know that administrators are supportive of their need to take care of themselves. Newman and Antonelli (2022) outlined basic policies schools and administrators can establish and follow on two levels:

Individual Level

- create a means of recognizing compassion fatigue or burnout on an individual level by gaining knowledge and awareness of the causes and potential exposure to it
- allow teachers a chance to slow down and focus on their needs
- allow teachers to find a work/life balance and act on it
- facilitate opportunities for teachers to build supportive connections with others

Setting Level (Schoolwide/District)

- create organizational and supervisory policies and practices that encourage self-care
- create supportive conditions and provide resources for teacher self-care
- provide professional development that teaches about self-care
- provide opportunities for peer support
- provide administrative support

These practices help to create a district culture of trauma-informed practices that go beyond supporting students to also supporting teachers, staff, and other community members.

Teacher Perceived Barrier: Preparedness for Trauma-Informed Practices

Every stage of the Missouri Model mentions the importance of embedding trauma-informed care or practices in the hiring processes for administrators, staff, and teachers. When organizations embed their values into each aspect of their operations, they are more likely to practice those values successfully. This is one of the tenets of change theory (Kotter, 2012). Living this premise by design is critical when creating a trauma-informed organization.

What this means to teachers, staff, and their administrators is that not only should those currently employed be trained at multiple levels and from multiple lenses about how to embed trauma-informed practices in their daily routines, but these values must also be embedded in the hiring processes. Employers and other academic stakeholders should demand that educator preparation programs (EPPs) incorporate trauma-informed practices and training in their curricula (L'Estrange & Howard, 2022). Education and awareness provide teachers with the tools to comprehend the impact of trauma on students.

Teachers with the necessary tools are more likely to address classroom issues appropriately. These tools include strategies such as implementing consistent and predictable classroom routines, using positive behavioral interventions and supports (PBIS), incorporating social-emotional learning (SEL) curricula, and utilizing appropriate de-escalation techniques to manage and reduce student distress effectively (Blodgett & Lanigan, 2018; Cole et al., 2013).

Recent research indicates that many pre-service educators feel inadequately prepared to implement trauma-informed principles or strategies during classroom disruptions (McClain, 2021). While teacher education programs often include basic classroom behavior management training, studies have found that educators frequently report a lack of confidence in applying trauma-informed practices effectively (Hobbs et al., 2019; McClain, 2021). For instance, a 2021 study, *Supporting Teachers from the Beginning by Preparing the Whole Teacher: Integrating Mindfulness and Social and Emotional Learning into Pre-Service Teacher Education,* revealed that pre-service teachers expressed a need for more comprehensive training to address the complexities of trauma-affected students (Hobbs et al., 2019). O'Toole and Dobutowitsch (2023) and Gherardi and Stoner (2024) noted that educators frequently feel unprepared to effectively implement trauma-informed practices in the classroom, emphasizing the critical need for targeted professional development.

Furthermore, even with some training exposure, educators struggle to implement in-class practice (Rahimi et al., 2021). Teachers want more training in child mental health needs (O'Toole & Dobutowitsch, 2023). Teachers must be proactive and advocate for more access to trauma-informed practice. Experts agree that a supportive community can help children overcome some trauma factors and lower the severity of the trauma response (Cole et al., 2013; Chafouleas et al., 2016). Therefore, teacher preparation programs should be rigorous in their training on trauma and trauma-informed classroom practices.

Creating a National Culture of Trauma-Informed Practices in Education

In 2019, Congresswoman Katherine Clark (D-MA-5), Congressman Mike Quigley (D-IL-5), and Congressman Brian Fitzpatrick (R-PA-1) introduced the Trauma-Informed Schools Act, which would have defined *trauma-informed practices* for the first time in federal education law. This bill would have also created key federal funding sources for teacher professional development and after-school programs. The goal of this bill was to provide educators with the training and resources they need to utilize trauma-informed care. However, this bill was not passed. In fact, it has been reintroduced both in the Senate or House several times. At the time of this writing, the latest version, *The Trauma-Informed Schools Act of 2024*, had been introduced and referred to the House Committee on Education and Workforce, but no other action has been taken (Trauma-Informed Schools Act, HR 8526, 2024). The original bill was designed to implement a schoolwide learning environment where all students and adults would feel safe, welcomed, and supported and could enable students to succeed despite traumatic experiences. Schools should provide services, support, and programs to meet individual student needs. These should be trauma-informed where appropriate and aim to increase student connection to the schoolwide learning environment. Additionally, schools should adopt disciplinary procedures and practices that accompany disciplinary actions with positive behavioral interventions to address the underlying causes of student behavior, including trauma. It is integral to avoid punitive or exclusionary disciplinary practices. Instead, schools should utilize evidence-based restorative practices that build a culture of trust. Such practices include facilitated dialogues and mediation sessions that focus on repairing harm and fostering understanding among students. This approach promotes an inclusive environment where all students have equitable access to education and support.

Considering that United States legislators seem reluctant to fund a trauma-informed schools act, as evidenced by the aforementioned bill being shuffled from committee to committee for the last five years, it is up to the states to legislate for the practices that research has shown are much needed. However, measuring efficacy is difficult. Rahimi et al. (2021) note that even if legislation is passed, there is no clear way of measuring how well educators adhere to trauma-informed best practices. Researchers would benefit by studying whether school districts across the country are implementing guidelines with fidelity. Increased funding for trauma-informed practices, smaller class sizes, additional counselors, and social workers would be beneficial to help address the needs of students who have experienced trauma. Still, we have yet to see this one aspect put into practice because bills such as the federal Trauma-Informed Schools Act keep being put on hold.

In 2011, Fallot published the *Creating Cultures of Trauma-Informed Care Fidelity Scale*. The scale provides a template for organizations and service agencies to assess their programs and how well they implement trauma-informed care. While this particular instrument is geared towards non-educational organizations, it would be relatively simple to modify it for academic settings. Considering Fallot and Harris' five core values of CCTI—safety, trustworthiness, choice, collaboration, and empowerment—a program can be said to be truly trauma-informed if these values are reflected in all of the following areas: each contact with individuals of the organization, the physical setting, relationships, and activities. Additionally, the trauma-informed culture should be evident in the experiences of staff (in education, that would be teachers, support staff, and administrators) as well as consumers (students and parents).

Conclusion

The profound impact of trauma on students' educational and social-emotional development necessitates a thorough approach to trauma-informed education. By recognizing and addressing the effects of adverse childhood experiences, educators and school communities can foster resilience, promote academic success, and facilitate healing. Integrating trauma-informed practices, as advocated by models such as the Missouri Model and Fallot and Harris' framework, highlights the importance of safety, trustworthiness, and empowerment within education settings. Continued investment in training, resources, and supportive policies is integral to maintaining these efforts and ensuring that all students have the opportunity to thrive despite a history of traumatic experiences.

References

Blodgett, C., & Lanigan, J. D. (2018). The association between adverse childhood experience (ACE) and school success in elementary school children. *School Psychology Quarterly, 33*(1), 137–146. https://doi.org/10.1037/spq0000256

Bridgland, V., Moeck, E., Green, D., Swain, T., Nayda, D., Matson, L., Hutchinson, N., & Takarangi, M. (2021). Why the COVID-19 pandemic is a traumatic stressor. *PLOS ONE*. https://doi.org/10.1371/journal.pone.0240146

Chafouleas, S. M., Johnson, A. H., Overstreet, S., & Santos, N. M. (2016). Toward a blueprint for trauma-informed service delivery in schools. *School Mental Health, 8*, 144-162. https://doi:10.1007/s12310-015-9166-9

Cole, S., Eisner, E., Gregory, M., & Ristuccia, J. (2013). A vision for a trauma-sensitive school. *Massachusetts Advocates for Children, 2*, 166–179.

Compassion Prison Project. (n.d.). Adverse childhood experiences (ACEs) in pris on populations. *Interrogating Justice*. https://interrogatingjustice.org/ending-mass-incarceration/adverse-childhood-events-more-common-among-adults-in-prison/

Duong, M. T., Nguyen, L., Gaias, L., Benjamin, K. S., Lee, K., Buntain-Ricklefs, J., & Cook, C. R. (2020). Using stakeholder input to guide cultural and contextual adaptations for a universal school-based intervention. *The Urban Review*. https://psycnet.apa.org/doi/10.1007/s11256-019-00547-w

Fallot, R. D., & Harris, M. (2011). *Creating cultures of trauma-informed care: Program self-assessment scale*. Community Connections.

Gherardi, S. A., & Stoner, A. (2024). Transcending attitudes: Teacher responses to professional development in trauma-informed education. *Discover Education, 3*(1), 132.

Grant, D. E., Jr., & Hill, J. B. (2020). Activating culturally empathic motivation in diverse students. *Journal of Education and Learning, 9*(5), 45–58. https://doi.org/10.5539/jel.v9n5p45

Harris, M. E., & Fallot, R. D. (2001). *Using trauma theory to design service systems*. Jossey-Bass/Wiley.

Heffernan, A., Bright, D., Kim, M., Longmuir, F., & Magyar, B. (2022). 'I cannot sustain the workload and the emotional toll': Reasons behind Australian teachers' intentions to leave the profession. *Australian Journal of Education, 66*(2), 196–209. https://doi.org/10.1177/00049441221086654

Hobbs, C., Paulsen, D., & Thomas, J. (2019). Trauma-informed practice for pre-service teachers. *Oxford Research Encyclopedia of Education*. https://doi.org/10.1093/acrefore/9780190264093.013.1435

Huang, L. N., Flatow, R., & Biggs, T. (2014). *SAMHSA's concept of trauma and guidance for a trauma-informed approach*. Substance Abuse and Mental Health Services Administration.

Jotkoff, E. (2022). NEA survey: Massive staff shortages in schools leading to educator burnout; alarming number of educators indicating they plan to leave profession. *National Education Association*. https://www.nea.org/about-nea/media-center/press-releases/nea-survey-massive-staff-shortages-schools-leading-educator-burnout-alarming-number-educators

Kotter, J. (2012). *Leading change*. Harvard Business Review Press.

Lander, J. (2018). Helping teachers manage the weight of trauma: Understanding and mitigating the effects of secondary traumatic stress for educators. *Harvard Graduate School of Education Usable Knowledge*. https://www.gse.harvard.edu/ideas/usable-knowledge/18/09/helping-teachers-manage-weight-trauma

L'Estrange, L., & Howard, J. (2022). Trauma-informed initial teacher education training: A necessary step in a system-wide response to addressing childhood trauma. *Frontiers in Education*, 7, Article 929582. https://doi.org/10.3389/feduc.2022.929582

McClain, M. P. (2021). Teacher candidates' perceptions of preparedness of teaching students who experience trauma. *Journal of Teacher Education and Educators, 10*(1), 5–23.

McGuire, L. (2024). Teachers need trauma-informed care, too. *Edutopia*.

Missouri Model for Trauma-Informed Schools. (2019). https://dmh.mo.gov/media/pdf/missouri-model-trauma-informed-schools

National Association of School Psychologists (NASP). (2024). Shortage of school psychologists. https://www.nasponline.org/research-and-policy/policy-priorities/critical-policy-issues/shortage-of-school-psychologists

National Education Association (NEA). (2024). Trauma-informed schools. https://www.nea.org/professional-excellence/student-engagement/trauma-informed-schools

Newman, L., & Antonelli, J. (2022). Building resilience among educators: A continuation high school shares strategies with its district to address compassion fatigue and secondary traumatic stress among teachers and staff. *Profiles in California Alternative Education*. https://files.eric.ed.gov/fulltext/ED618203.pdf

Ormiston, H. E., Nygaard, M. A., & Apgar, S. (2022). A systematic review of secondary traumatic stress and compassion fatigue in teachers. *School Mental Health, 14*(4), 802–817. https://doi.org/10.1007/s12310-022-09525-2

O'Toole, C., & Dobutowitsch, M. (2023). The courage to care: Teacher compassion predicts more positive attitudes toward trauma-informed practice. *Journal of Child & Adolescent Trauma, 16*(1), 123–133. https://doi.org/10.1007/s40653-022-00486-x

Owens, M., Thornbrough, K., & Yakimowski, M. E. (2023). A case study which explores the mindsets of students placed in residential care home and perceptions of their teachers. *Samford University*. https://files.eric.ed.gov/fulltext/EJ1322108.pdf

Rahimi, R., Liston, D. D., Adkins, A., & Nourzad, J. (2021). Teacher awareness of trauma-informed practice: Raising awareness in Southeast Georgia. *Georgia Educational Researcher, 18*(2), 72.

Roeder, K. M. (2021). *Exploring trauma-informed education in teacher preparation and the prevalence of trauma-informed indicators in pre-service educators' classroom behavior management plans*. Pilot Study. Fontbonne University. Unpublished manuscript.

Roeder, K. M. (2022). *Examining educators' perceived impact of trauma-informed training and professional development in the classroom and related classroom behavior management practices* (Publication No. 553). Fontbonne University. *All Theses, Dissertations, and Capstone Projects*. https://griffinshare.fontbonne.edu/all-etds/553

Sharkey, J. D., Mullin, A., Felix, E. D., & Rodriguez, S. (2024). Supporting educators and students: A university–community partnership to implement trauma-informed practices in schools. *School Mental Health, 16*, 879–893. https://doi.org/10.1007/s12310-024-09667-5

Substance Abuse Mental Health Services Administration (SAMHSA). (2021). *Understanding child trauma*. https://www.samhsa.gov/child-trauma/understanding-child-trauma

Trauma-Informed Schools Act of 2024, H.R. 8526, 118th Congress (2023–2024). https://www.congress.gov/bill/118th-congress/house-bill/8526/text

Walker, T. (2019). "I didn't know it had a name": Secondary traumatic stress and educators. *NEA Today*. https://www.nea.org/nea-today/all-news-articles/i-didnt-know-it-had-name-secondary-traumatic-stress-and-educators

World Health Organization (WHO). (2020). Child maltreatment. https://www.who.int/news-room/fact-sheets/detail/child-maltreatment

CHAPTER 10

Developing A University Peer Support Allies Program to Address Student Mental Health

Amy Ruffus-Doerr

Introduction

The youth mental health crisis that began in 2009 has continued to worsen over the past 16 years, with over half of college students meeting the criteria for at least one mental illness (Department of Health and Human Services, 2022; LeViness et al., 2019; Lipson et al., 2022). Traditional therapy and on-campus counseling centers cannot cope with the demand and are underutilized by traditionally marginalized populations. Developing a peer-centered program, the Peer Support Allies (PSAs), can help with this crisis (SAMHSA, n.d.; Mead et al., 2001). The PSAs represent a diverse student body and are trained to provide mental health referral support, reduce the stigma of having mental health needs, model healthy behaviors, and provide a solution to overwhelmed and under-representative counseling centers. The PSA program is grounded in the socio-ecological model and addresses community, campus, peer, and individual issues. This chapter outlines the development and implementation of a PSA program and steps for program evaluation. By leveraging the power of peers to influence one another and fostering a group of more representative allies, a PSA program can increase a sense of belonging on campus and reduce barriers to mental health support.

No Reserves to Cope

Teaching in-person classes in late 2020 was daunting. As the fall semester began, I was taken aback by the overwhelming number of mental health issues my students were experiencing. Previously, they had coped with varying degrees of success, but their issues emerged with the stress of the COVID-19 pandemic. Daily, I was approached by students dealing with overwhelming levels of anxiety, depression, and loneliness. Others struggled with the repercussions of a sexual assault or the stress of supporting friends with suicidal thoughts. While these mental health issues are not new for students, the intensity and urgency of students' feelings were startling. It was as if they had no reserves to cope. Students who were willing to see a mental health professional often encountered obstacles such as finding a therapist, understanding which therapy options were appropriate for them, and navigating financial and insurance barriers, not to mention the time-consuming process of finding a therapist with whom they could truly connect.

Students needed help, yet they turned toward me or friends instead of seeking professional help. As a kind of triage, I often asked them how much their issues negatively impacted their life. Most students were so overwhelmed that they could barely function. However, when I suggested we walk over to our campus counseling center or that I would help them make an appointment with a therapist, they would repeat the often cited, "It's not bad enough to get counseling," or "I'd rather talk to you or my friends." This dichotomy confounded me, but eventually, it became obvious that they saw therapy as crisis intervention, a last resort. Many also didn't feel represented in psychology, often citing deeply rooted cultural fears around mental health and a feeling of being misunderstood or even abused by the discipline. Further probing students, asking why they came to me instead of a licensed professional, the response was repeatedly: "You already know me. I don't need to start at the beginning with you," or "I know I can trust that you'll get it." When a colleague expressed the same experiences with students, we knew a bigger-picture solution was necessary. After researching, we were surprised to find the extent of the mental health crisis and began researching alternative solutions. We came upon the idea of a Peer

Educator as an option, but it didn't quite suit the needs of our students. We didn't need educators in this mental health crisis; we needed trained allies.

The Surging Student Mental Health Crisis

As early as 2009, researchers sounded the alarm that the mental health of adolescents and young adults was getting progressively worse and not better. Many see teachers as first responders, the primary point of contact for their students' mental health. But are they the best contact points, or is it convenient? Because teachers are not mental health professionals, they may lack the expertise and resources to identify and support a student in need, with some students falling through the cracks. Teachers are often aware of this gap and experience heightened levels of stress due to a mismatch between their perceived responsibility of caring for their students' mental health and their limited training in the field (Ekornes, 2017). It is a vicious cycle. When negative interactions between teachers and students increase, so does teachers' and students' perceived stress. Though many teachers desire to help, they don't have the training or the resources.

This mental health crisis is far too big a problem for teachers to handle alone. As stated earlier, and as of 2023, over half of college students in the United States met the criteria for at least one mental health issue (Lipson et al., 2022). In response, the US Surgeon General called on institutions to lead a quick collaborative response to address the crisis where a shocking 80% of those suffering do not seek help. He also felt it necessary to empower "youth ... to recognize, manage, and learn from difficult emotions" (Department of Health and Human Services, 2022, p. 1). In 2023, the Healthy Minds Study released data for the last ten years showing a 19% increase in depression, a 19% increase in anxiety, and a 6% increase in suicidal ideation in adolescents and young adults. Emergency room visits for suicide attempts went up 51% for young girls (Curtin, 2020; US Surgeon General Advisory Board, 2021), yet shockingly, over 50% of those who experience suicidal ideation do not seek help.

As students struggled to cope, so did the adult population. About half of all adults reported that stress from the COVID-19 pandemic had made planning and looking toward the future impossible. A third admitted they struggled to make fundamental decisions such as dressing and feeding themselves (American Psychological Association [APA], 2023). Unfortunately, this is not just a pandemic problem. With the easing of lockdown restrictions, teachers expected a dramatic increase in student engagement and moods. Both student *and* teacher self-reports show continued academic and social disengagement (Hartocollis, 2021) and further decreasing mental health (Healthy Minds, 2023). The lingering effects of inconsistent lockdown restrictions left students anxious, isolated, and depressed.

Traditionally, teachers, parents, and staff turn to school counselors and campus mental health services, but they, too, are overwhelmed. Since 2018, college campus counseling centers have reported a steady increase in demand without any increase in funding or staff (LeViness et al., 2019), leaving them overworked and understaffed. As the pandemic took hold, high schools also saw a steady decline in student mental health. A total of 60% of high school principals report depression as a severe problem, 72% say most of their students have problems with social and emotional issues, and a whopping 75% report referring students for mental health services (Kaufman et al., 2016). While post-secondary institutions have not seen an increase in budgets for counseling services, then-Vice President Kamala Harris increased the budget to hire and train 14,000 K–12 school counselors in early 2023 (Gangitano, 2024). But is it enough? Understaffed and underfunded, counseling centers on secondary and post-secondary campuses have shifted from providing routine and preventative mental health care to crisis counseling. Increasingly, their sessions with students center around acute crisis issues such as suicidal ideation, assault, and drug abuse. Students frequently struggle for a considerable time before reaching out for assistance, and the limited availability of counselors allows them to provide only short-term support. If traditional counseling services miss 80% of those in need, maybe it is time to consider novel models.

Reaching the Resistant with Peer-Led Programs

Given the importance of peers in adolescence and young adulthood (Erickson, 1950; Abdi & Simbar, 2013), it is not surprising that this group instinctively rejects any influence from authority, and members look to one another as a natural source of support and behavioral models (Cruz, 2019; Abdi & Simbar, 2013). This perspective positions peers to reduce stigmatization by normalizing healthy and help-seeking behaviors. This may be especially helpful for students from traditionally marginalized populations, including racial, ethnic, and sexual minorities, who are more difficult to reach with traditional therapy. They are also less likely to be diagnosed, less likely to use medication, and less likely to attend therapy. However, they are at a more elevated risk for suicide relative to the general population (Lipson et al., 2018). Peers will never replace therapists, but they can become a component of a proactive movement on mental health and well-being by reducing barriers to mental health support.

Reducing Barriers with Peer Allies

It is unusual for an adolescent or young adult to ask an adult for help, which positions peer approaches especially relevant in this mental health crisis (Cruz, 2019). Peer support is best known for its role in addiction recovery, where peers show the powerful impact of a shared understanding and mutual sense of empowerment (SAMHSA, n.d.; Mead et al., 2001). Drawing inspiration from this model, the Peer Support Allies prioritize respect and belonging and model healthy choices as the foundation for help-seeking behavior. When peers come from similar socioeconomic backgrounds, it establishes them as a reliable and trustworthy extension of the community, which reduces any power dynamic that may inhibit further help-seeking behaviors and may engage students who would not traditionally feel accepted in a therapeutic setting (Cornell University, 2020). They advocate for people, share useful skills and resources, and help build a support community. However, it must be noted that PSAs are not crisis interventionists or peer counselors.

Addressing Representation

Because PSAs represent students from varied socioeconomic, gender, racial, and religious backgrounds, they may be able to identify students needing help but who historically slip through the cracks in traditional counseling. Compared to their peers from higher socioeconomic backgrounds, adolescents and young adults belonging to families that have a low socioeconomic status are two-to-three times more likely to develop mental health conditions and are less likely to seek help (Reiss, 2013). When PSAs are representative of the student population, they are well placed to increase diversity and representation in mental health issues that commonly delay the utilization of mental health services. The aim is to encourage social connectedness, eliminate the stigma associated with mental health problems, and foster healthy habits using the *for us, by us* approach.

Lessons Learned Through Developing a Peer Support Ally Program

Creating our own PSA program from scratch was an incredibly daunting task, and unfortunately, few models were available, leading to many learning moments as we developed the program. The most common and impactful topics needing review revolved around appropriate student behavior, team roles, how to handle conflict, and useful training programs. For our PSA pilot program to be consistent, the first step was to outline policy and procedures in a PSA program manual. The manual includes the following topics: a theoretical approach, recruiting students and stakeholders, training programs, assessing the needs, committees, groups, forms, and procedures. The most difficult areas in the process for our pilot program centered around the group dynamics of the PSAs and around articulating specific procedures and processes for anticipated conflicts and problems. The following sections outline all the lessons learned throughout the process, which can serve as a model for other programs.

Using the Socio-Ecological Model as a Base for the PSA Program

A well-rounded Peer Support Ally program should address mental health and wellness at all levels of the socio-ecological model. The socio-ecological model, developed by Bronfenbrenner (1979), considers the complex interactions between individuals and the social world. The interplay of these systems is examined to understand how they impact adolescents' and young adults' mental health and wellness. Bronfenbrenner divided the outwardly expanding spheres of influence into the microsystem, mesosystem, exosystem, and macrosystem. Adjusting the framework to program needs, we identified the microsystem as a community (policy), the mesosystem as a campus (organizational), the exosystem as a peer (interpersonal), and the macrosystem as a student (intrapersonal), as shown in Figure 10.1.

Figure 10.1
Peer Support Ally Levels of the Socio-Ecological Model

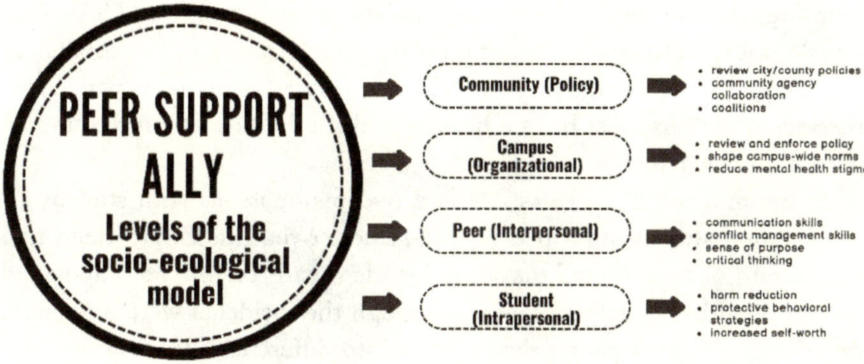

This model allows for the full range of factors that can impact a student on a personal and societal level. It also suggests that interventions must be across multiple levels to be effective. Overarching issues in the community, which include social-historical conditions such as the Black Lives Matter movement or the racial protests that erupted globally in 2020, can impact students' mental health as much as do interpersonal concerns such as a divorce. Peer-led programs may help students process world events (community policy) to address the impact on the student's home life (student interpersonal).

Recruiting Students and Stakeholders

Choosing PSAs peer allies should be a highly selective process. Training PSAs is a time-intensive process requiring students to complete at least one full academic year as a PSA. Paying peer allies for their work was much more difficult than initially expected, and we fell far short of the number of PSAs we needed. Grants were not a consistent and reliable source of income.

Aligning the PSA program goals to a class is a more consistent way to feed the program with new PSAs each year, minimizing the need to recruit students and find annual revenue streams. PSAs are meant to represent the student population, so they must have a range of interests, experiences, and backgrounds. Although we did not initially anticipate problems with the class recruitment model, serious flaws should be noted. One significant drawback is that not every student enrolled in a course will be well-suited to be a PSA, nor will they be interested in becoming a peer ally. Those who are still too deep in their mental health struggles, addictions, and unhealthy relationships did not model the healthy choices we expected from PSAs. Peer allies do not need to be perfect but must be willing to seek professional help when necessary. While the peer model indicates that a shared experience is necessary, the PSAs must be in a healthy and stable state of mind to model appropriate behaviors.

In the first round of PSAs, we had two major issues with student allies. The first student informed us mid-semester that his ex-girlfriend had accused him of assault, and the second student had recently been abducted and assaulted by an acquaintance. Although the incidents were unrelated, our priority was to separate the students into different subcommittees and never hold meetings where both would attend. This was to ensure the female assault survivor felt safe in the program. The student accused of assault was immediately taken off any public duties related to the program, had no interactions with other students, and spent his hours on administrative tasks until the case went before a judge, as at the time, it was a charge and not a conviction. Within a few weeks, the charges were dropped, and after much debate, it was decided that it would not be beneficial for the program to have him as a PSA, so he was moved to research and grant writing, having interactions with the faculty only. The second student, who survived a sexual assault and harrowing abduction, understandably had difficulties with her mental health. We believed being around other students as a model didn't benefit her or the PSA program. Instead, this student developed a database of community resources in the local area that would be beneficial to partner with.

After these two experiences, we adjusted the class model of recruitment by having multiple options available for students who were enrolled in a course but were not interested or were not a good fit for the PSA program. For example, one student trained (virtually) and was on call for a public crisis text line instead of working as a PSA. Although this is a less-than-ideal circumstance, the crisis text line allowed the student who had a reputation on campus as a loafer and would not have been a good model for other students to complete the objectives of the class. Another student in a similar circumstance worked virtually for a local nonprofit on their social media campaigns. Presenting these options within the PSA program allowed us to choose the students more intentionally.

Establishing Interdepartmental Collaboration

Interdepartmental collaboration is a necessity, as financial resources and time constraints will make the program development, implementation, and sustainability too large for one staff or faculty member. A collaboration of Student Affairs, Academic Affairs, and interdepartmental collaboration can increase the program's sustainability, development, implementation, and evaluation and help the program recruit a broader range of students. However, the needs and regulations of each department may conflict. To avoid this, we divided the duties by committee (*healthy relationships* or *mental health stigma*) so each group had a clear area of expertise and was responsible for a specific committee of PSAs. Students, faculty, and staff do not need prior training or experience in psychology but should be prepared to demonstrate why they would be a strong peer support ally.

Developing the Training Programs

Prior to starting as Peer Support Allies, students, faculty, and staff need to be trained on various topics. These include Title IX, the Family Educational Rights and Privacy Act (FERPA), active listening, interpersonal identities, confidentiality vs. anonymity, setting healthy boundaries, accessing professional and community resources, maintaining one's mental health, and the mental health resources and procedures available at the school. When creating the Peer Support Allies pilot program, there was no single training course that covered all the topics, so it became necessary to use multiple training courses. In addition, we found training in group formation, roles, and styles to be imperative. While using different training programs to cover all topics was necessary, it was not time-efficient. Each student invested around 40 hours or around five weeks of class time to complete all the training. After each training course was completed, PSAs were given a post-training, self-reporting assessment consisting of questions to help assess a PSA's confidence on topics surrounding student mental health, time management, communication skills, managing conflicts, self-care, and crisis intervention. Because PSAs come from diverse backgrounds with different prior knowledge, misconceptions will vary. This post-training questionnaire allowed us to see what gaps in knowledge still existed, what was redundant, what they learned, and what they still needed to know. Emerging themes told us that PSAs wanted to practice the skills more, that video scenarios in the courses lacked believability, and that all felt overly simplified. PSAs were concerned that the training did not offer the ambiguity and complexity they felt in real-life scenarios.

Be There training.

One promising curriculum we found was *Be There* training, created in partnership with Jack.org and the Born This Way Foundation. The *Be There* certificate is a free, digital, self-paced learning experience designed to increase mental health literacy and provide youth with the knowledge, skills, and confidence they need to safely support anyone struggling with their mental health (Be There, n.d.). This free training is offered in three languages and is designed to help people recognize when a person is struggling, the trainee's role as a support, and how to connect them with appropriate resources. It also addresses the intersection of culture and identity in mental health and wellness. The modules are interactive with simulated texting, videos, and pretests. The topics include how to recognize signs of struggle, what to say to start the conversation, how to build trust and offer practical support, tips to become a better listener, the importance of setting healthy boundaries, how to help someone access professional and community resources, and how to maintain your mental health. Each module begins with a summary of the topic and a quick pretest. Next is a video, with a transcription of two people discussing or recounting an incident related to the overall topic. Third is an AI-simulated text conversation where the user can interact with predetermined prompts to apply the information from this section. Finally, there is a further reading and post-test section.

Creating and Maintaining Successful Groups

One of the major challenges in implementing a PSA program is forming cohesive groups that can effectively resolve conflicts and distribute the workload equally. Because students will come from diverse backgrounds, a period to develop group cohesion and identity is necessary. Tuckman & Jensen's (1977) *stages of group development of forming, storming, norming, performing, adjourning, and next steps* are useful for understanding the group formation process and outlining anticipated behaviors for each stage.

During the first stage, forming, group members are high energy, have high expectations for the group's success, and focus on creating goals and direction for the group. During storming, the second stage, group members become frustrated with one another, and the process and experience conflict. Disagreements will emerge at this stage between group members as frustration mounts and they question their abilities to meet the goals. Practicing conflict management skills learned through training may be necessary. Norming is the third stage in group development. Group members begin to resolve conflicts and compromise, feel a sense of shared responsibility and identity to the group, and feel comfortable sharing ideas and working together even when it is a compromise. You will see a decrease in anxiety and an increase in group cohesion. In the performing stage, the group members trust one another and are motivated to produce deliverable content that serves the project's greater goals. They demonstrate the ability to self-manage and deal effectively with conflict. Members encourage collective problem-solving and celebrate group success. Finally, in the adjourning stage, group members look for closure after completing the project. Some members may be sad and miss one another, while others will be burnt out and feel a sense of relief. While establishing group cohesiveness is an expected and predictable process, setting norms, roles, and goals can decrease frustration and offer a roadmap out of conflict.

Establishing Cohesiveness, Group Norms, and Roles

This stage of the PSA program development was significantly more complex than we had expected. As the first group of PSAs went through training and initial program planning, cracks in group communication and expectations began to show from day one. One of the biggest takeaways from the first year was that all roles, expectations, and procedures must be created by the group and explicitly stated. Clarity and definitions are of the utmost importance and are a simple but profound way to avoid frustration and unnecessary conflict. For example, while moderating a PSA meeting, it became obvious that each student had a completely different understanding of the phrase *last minute*. One student felt it meant just minutes before the program started, while another felt it meant working on tasks days before the due date. In moments of frustration, these misunderstandings led them to ascribe negative characteristics to their groupmates including, "he's lazy, a loafer," and "she is controlling and a perfectionist." When we realized the problem was clarifying our definitions, tediously laying out explicit expectations became the priority and solution to the group issues.

To have a structured conversation about conflicts within the group, we had each PSA group work through The Five Conflict Handling Modes by Thomas and Kilmann (2008). This model assesses how people react to and work through conflict on two dimensions: assertiveness and cooperativeness (see Figure 10.2).

Figure 10.2
The Five Conflict Handling Modes by Thomas and Kilmann (2008)

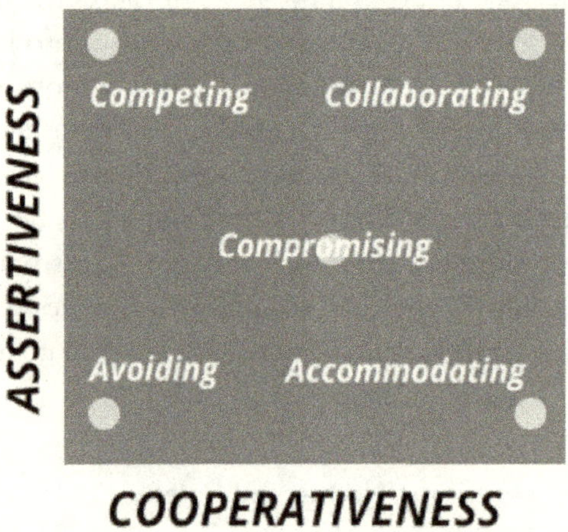

Note: Assertiveness and cooperativeness, two dimensions of human behavior, can be used to define what Thomas and Kilmann describe as these five different modes of responding to conflict: competing, collaborating, compromising, avoiding, and accommodating. Figure has been modified from original figure with permission. Original figure is available at: http://www.kilmanndiagnostics.com/overview-thomas-kilmann-conflict-mode-instrument-tki

Based on one's level of the two dimensions (assertiveness and cooperativeness), they created five conflict modes: competing, collaborating, compromising, avoiding, and accommodating. A competing group member focuses on their needs and competes for authority in the group. A person who falls into the collaborating mode of handling conflicts works to find a solution that satisfies all the group members. Compromising students find a quick solution that somewhat satisfies all group members. An avoiding style does not express their thoughts and sidesteps any disagreement. Finally, the accommodating group members sacrifice their own needs for that of the group.

While our PSAs didn't likely dramatically change their approach to conflict, we found that going through this mode of conflict as a group, identifying the primary mode for each member, and discussing strategies moving forward were useful. It also allowed them to think about how each member handled conflict. If a PSA noticed the avoider giving in at the first sign of conflict, it reminded the students to check in with them. This check-in usually came from a teacher as the students worked on their conflict intelligence.

After establishing conflict styles, we established roles within the committees by assigning each PSA one of the following roles: scribe, conflict mediator, leader, and head of communication (see Table 10.1).

Table 10.1
Group Roles

Role	Questions to Answer	Process When Roles are not Maintained
Scribe	What style, format, and level of detail for meeting notes will be used?	Who contacts the scribe, and on what platform?
Conflict Mediator	How will we lay out the progressive steps for conflict resolution?	What are your expectations of the mediator during the conflict? Include an acceptable response time.
Leader	What leadership style do we need?	How involved do we expect the leader to be in day-to-day and overarching tasks?
Head of Communication	What is our accepted response time? Immediate, 12 hours, one day?	

The scribe was responsible for taking meeting notes, emailing members, and making the notes available to the group within one day of the meeting. The questions the PSAs discussed as a group for this role were style, format, mode of distribution, and level of detail for meeting notes. In year two, the scribe of one committee failed to consistently post meeting summaries and to-do lists within the group's pre-agreed timeline. The students' first instinct was to tell a faculty member and suggest a punishment. The faculty redirected the students to the mediator, who acted as the contact point for conflicts within the group. Preferably, this person would score as a collaborator on The Five Conflict Handling Modes (Thomas & Kilmann, 2008), making them both high on assertiveness and cooperativeness.

As a group, the PSAs detailed progressive steps for conflict resolution and expectations of the mediator during conflict. For the leadership role, as a group, they defined what kind of leader they needed on their committee and how involved the leader needed to be in day-to-day and overarching tasks. This needed to be explicit and concrete to avoid further conflict. For example, the lead PSA checked in via text 24 hours before an event to ascertain if all the needs for the event had been met; if not, they requested a detailed schedule (including a time stamp) of when each task would be complete, along with an update text four hours before the event. If the student was not responsive after eight hours, only then did the lead PSA check in with the faculty.

The head of communications was responsible for strengthening the group's communication boundaries and moderating group discussions on topics such as what acceptable response time is and what procedures there are if someone fails to meet those expectations. The PSAs also specified procedures if the committee members did not complete their duties as detailed. Establishing clear expectations in painstaking detail was incredibly helpful in addressing group dynamics. Our PSAs tended to go to a faculty member for leadership and conflict resolution, but with these defined roles, we could redirect the issue to the appropriate PSA and offload those tasks. There were inevitable conflicts around response time and the fairness of the workload. While these procedures and rules did not eliminate conflict, they kept the overachiever from dominating the project and gave a clear, nonconfrontational way to address these issues.

Creating Policy, Procedures, and Forms

The University Program Development Manual for Peer Support Allies (Caine & Ruffus-Doerr, 2021) outlines explicit principles, program standards, and ethics (Appendix A). This ensures institutional memory and consistency in the program, even as faculty, staff, and students leave and join. For our program, we outlined three major principles: ethical practice, cultivating well-being, and a community-based approach. The PSA program practice standards are adapted from the American College Health Association's guidelines for health promotion. They are guided by the following principles: alignment with the mission of the organization, socio-ecological-based practice, collaboration, inclusive practice, and evidence-informed practice. Under each of these standards, we articulated expectations for the PSAs, and they also read and signed this document upon hire. Our PSA code of ethics (Appendix B) outlines expectations and serves as a contract between the PSA and the program coordinator. We required each PSA to sign this form before they began working on the program and provided them with a copy.

Conclusion

Researchers have been warning that the mental health of adolescents and young adults is consistently declining. Because so many students who need help with mental health issues are not seeking it, a huge population is struggling without support or tools. Increasing the number of counselors would help but still would not reach those students who are resistant to therapy and fear being stigmatized. Novel approaches, similar to the Peer Support Allies, could help bridge the gap and support those who would otherwise suffer independently. Creating a Peer Support Allies program can be daunting, but Peer Support Allies could be an effective tool to combat the mental health crisis on school grounds.

References

Abdi, F., & Simbar, M. (2013). The peer education approach in adolescents-narrative review article. *Iranian journal of public health*, *42*(11), 1200–1206.

American Psychological Association. (2023, November). *Stress in America 2023: A nation recovering from collective trauma* [Press release]. https://www.apa.org/news/press/releases/stress/2023/collective-trauma-recovery

Be There Certificate. (n.d.). *Earn your Be There certificate.* https://www.betherecetificate.org/

Bronfenbrenner, U. (1979). *The ecology of human development: Experiments by nature and design.* Harvard University Press.

Caine, J., & Ruffus-Doerr, A. (2021). Program development manual: Fontbonne certified peer educators program [Unpublished manual] Department of biological and behavioral sciences, Fontbonne University.

Cornell University. (2020). Mental health review: Final Report. https://mentalhealth.cornell.edu/sites/mentalhealth/files/2022-09/Cornell_MHR-Final-Report_4-15-20_Final.pdf

Cruz, M. K. (2019, May 27). Crowdsourcing Mental Health. https://clalliance.org/blog/crowdsourcing-mental-health/

Curtin, S. C. (2020). State suicide rates among adolescents and young adults aged 10–24: United States, 2000–2018.

Department of Health and Human Services. (2022). Mental health annual report: 2015-2020 https://www.samhsa.gov/data/sites/default/files/reports/rpt38666

/2020_MH-CLD%20Annual%20Report-508%20compliant_10212022_final.pdf

Ekornes, S. (2017) Teacher stress related to student mental health promotion: The match between perceived demands and competence to help students with mental health problems. *Scandinavian Journal of Educational Research*, *61*(3), 333–353. https://doi.org/10.1080/00313831.2016.1147068

Erikson, E. H. (1950). *Childhood and society*. WW Norton & Company.

Gangitano, A. (2024, January 11). Harris announces $285M to boost mental health counselors in schools. *The Hill*. https://thehill.com/homenews/administration/4402821-harris-announces-285m-to-boost-mental-health-counselors-in-schools/

Hartocollis, A. (2021, December 22) Another surge in the virus has colleges fearing a mental health crisis. *The New York Times*. https://www.nytimes.com/2021/12/22/us/covid-college-mental-health-suicide.html

Healthy Minds Network (2023). Healthy Minds Study among Colleges and Universities, 2022–2023. Healthy Minds Network, University of Michigan, University of California Los Angeles, Boston University, and Wayne State University. https://healthymindsnetwork.org/research/data-for-researchers

Kaufman, J. H., Seelam, R., Woodbridge, M. W., Sontag-Padilla, L., Osilla, K. C., & Stein, B. D. (2016). Student mental health in California's K–12 schools. *US National Library of Medicine National Institutes of Health*. https://www.rand.org/content/dam/rand/pubs/research_reports/RR1100/RR1129/RAND_RR1129.pdf

LeViness, P., Bershad, C., Gorman, K. Braun, L., & Murray, T. (2019). The association for university and college counseling center directors annual survey. https://www.aucccd.org/assets/documents/Survey/2018%20aucccd%20survey-public-revised.pdf

Lipson, S. K., Kern, A., Eisenberg, D., & Breland-Noble, A. M. (2018). Mental health disparities among college students of color. *Journal of Adolescent Health*, *63*(3), 348–356.

Lipson, S. K., Zhou, S., Abelson, S., Heinze, J., Jirsa, M., Morigney, J., Patterson, A., Singh, M., & Eisenberg, D. (2022). Trends in college student mental health and help-seeking by race/ethnicity: Findings from the national healthy minds study, 2013–2021. *Journal of Affective Disorders*, *306*, 138–147.

Mead, S., Hilton, D., & Curtis, L. (2001). Peer support: A theoretical perspective. *Psychiatric Rehabilitation Journal*, *25*(2), 134–141. https://doi.org/10.1037/h0095032

Reiss, F. (2013). Socioeconomic inequalities and mental health problems in children and adolescents: A systematic review. *Social Science & Medicine*, *90*, 24–31. https://doi.org/10.1016/j.socscimed.2013.04.026

SAMHSA. (n.d.) *Peer support workers for those in recovery*. https://www.samhsa.gov/brss-tacs/recovery-support-tools/peers

Thomas, K. W. & Kilmann, R. H. (2008). Thomas-Kilmann conflict mode instrument. *TKI profile and interpretive report, 1*(11). https://lig360.com/wp-content/uploads/2022/09/Conflict-Styles-Assessment.pdf

Tuckman, B. W., & Jensen, M. A. C. (1977). Stages of small-group development revisited. *Group & Organization Studies*, 2(4), 419–427. https://doi.org/10.1177/105960117700200404

US Surgeon General Advisory Board. (2021). *Protecting Youth Mental Health*. https://www.hhs.gov/sites/default/files/surgeon-general-youth-mental-health-advisory.pdf

Appendix A

The University Program Development Manual for Peer Support Allies

PSA Program Principles

Principle 1: Ethical Practice

It is critical that PSA leaders and student volunteers conduct their work in an ethical manner and expect and encourage the same of their colleagues.

Principle 2: Cultivate Well-Being and Student Success

PSAs cultivate well-being and student success by working to prevent personal and community mental health concerns. PSAs honor the personalized definition of well-being and respect community members' autonomy while promoting a definition that includes mental health and wellness, connection with the greater community, connection with education, and access to resources.

Principle 3: Community-Based Approach

PSAs identify their schools as a community. Students, staff, faculty, alumni, and community collaborators engage with the school, and thus have a shared identity as members of the community. PSAs understand that change within the community is made possible by its collective identity. PSA programming will utilize a community-based approach, which builds upon the community members' relationships and community systems, to promote positive change.

PSA Program Standards

The PSA program practice standards are adapted from the American College Health Association's guidelines for health promotion in higher education. The PSA standards of practice are guided by the following principles.

Standard 1: Alignment with the Mission of Your Organization

Effective mental health and wellness promotion practice require the PSA program to align its values with your organization's missions.

Standard 2: Socio-Ecological Based Practice

Effective practice of mental health promotion requires the PSA program to address campus and community health and well-being at all levels of the socioecological model.

PSAs agree to

1. Advocate for the use of the socioecological model as the foundation for efforts promoting campus health and well-being and use data from their community to better understand the need.
2. Plan, implement, and evaluate initiatives that address the interpersonal and population-level influences on mental health and well-being.
3. Advocate for campus, local, state, and national policies that influence campus and community health and well-being.

Standard 3: Collaboration

Effective practice of health promotion PSA program requires a shared responsibility of all campus and community members to enhance health and well -being.

PSAs will

1. Identify and collaborate with interdisciplinary partners, including students, faculty, staff, administrators, and community partners that support mental health.
2. Engage with campus and community organizations to maximize the reach of the PSA program.

Standard 4: Inclusive Practice

Effective practice of mental health promotion requires the PSA program to demonstrate cultural humility and inclusivity.

PSAs will

1. Design data implemented mental health promotion initiatives driven by the values of inclusion, respect, and equity for marginalized populations.

2. Design, implement, and assess best practices informed by the distinct needs of a diverse population.

Standard 5: Theory-Based Practice

Effective practice of health promotion of a PSA program is to understand and apply accepted interdisciplinary theoretical frameworks and planning models that address the well-being of the community.

PSAs will

1. Review professional resources and literature from interdisciplinary sources on theoretical frameworks and planning models.

2. Assess how theories are successfully applied to program initiatives, and modify as needed.

Standard 6: Evidence-Informed Practice

Effective practice of health promotion of a PSA program is to understand and utilize evidence to inform health promotion processes and initiatives.

PSAs will

1. Review published research with demonstrated efficacy that will inform mental health promotion initiatives.

2. Develop measurable goals and objectives for the mental health promotion processes and implement evidence-informed processes and initiatives.

3. Share assessment and evaluation findings with the campus, community, and the field.

PSA signature ______________________________ Date ______________

Appendix B

Peer Support Ally Code of Ethics

I value and know my role as a peer ally. To best fulfill that role, I will:

1. Serve as a bridge between students and the professional resources available on campus or in the surrounding community.
2. Commit to not exploit any situation or take advantage of someone's vulnerability for my personal gain.
3. I will respect confidentiality, except in situations where I determine the person is at risk of physical or mental harm or discloses information that I must report in accordance with the law or campus regulations.
4. I will offer only information that I am qualified to offer and with the greatest accuracy possible.
5. Strive to transform the campus and community environment so that it will encourage healthy decision-making. I will not provide services beyond my training.

I recognize the importance of my mental well-being. To fulfill this responsibility, I will:

1. Acknowledge that my top priority is my own mental health.
2. Avoid letting my peer support ally obligations interfere with my personal goals and will not put my emotional, mental, or physical health at risk.

I acknowledge and appreciate my role as a team member. To fulfill it effectively, I will:

1. Embrace supervision and assistance from my advisor and teammates.

2. Actively engage in the peer ally program.

3. Encourage and support my fellow peer allies.

As a peer ally, I acknowledge my role. To effectively carry out this role, I commit to:

1. Treat individuals with respect and dignity.

2. Embrace diversity in all its forms.

3. Realize that every person is continuously evolving and learning, and therefore, I will be patient and understanding.

____

Signature

____

Print Name

CHAPTER 11

The Journey Toward Becoming *Truly* Trauma-Informed

Jamie Doronkin and Joanne Fish

Becoming *Truly* Trauma-Informed

This last chapter serves as both a conclusion and a collection of ideas on what educators, schools, and school districts can do to become *truly* trauma-informed. In essence, it provides elements of what one might call an organizational improvement plan (OIP). We do not attempt to outline an OIP because we recognize that this might look different for each school building. What we hope we have done is provide insights, ideas, and resources educators and future educators can use to improve their schools and their own statuses as being trauma-informed.

As chapter authors have noted in various ways, schools and their districts are not *truly* trauma-informed until every facet of their day-to-day work is representative of and acts on what that means. According to the Missouri Model framework for Trauma-Informed Approaches (2019), being *truly* trauma-informed requires a "profound paradigm shift in knowledge, perspective, attitudes and skills that continues to deepen and unfold over time" (para. 1). These perspectives, attitudes, and skills must be prevalent in every facet and action of an organization. They should be embedded in the culture of a trauma-informed organization, including in its hiring practices.

So, what could being *truly* trauma-informed look like? Trauma-informed organizations might include interview questions that pertain to being trauma-informed; they would provide both onboard training and continuing education that pertain to being trauma-informed, and they would make allowances in employees' workdays to promote trauma-informed activities. For example, a school/school district that is trauma-informed would seek out teacher candidates who have been educated on trauma-informed practices in their educator preparation programs. During interviews, they might ask potential candidates about how they might handle scenarios requiring trauma-informed approaches and skills. Their new-teacher training would include information on how their district manages incidents that require trauma-informed approaches, explaining the steps teachers should take when trauma-related situations require intervention, or on how to recognize students' actions that stem from trauma or toxic stress. Building administrators would ensure that teachers and support staff are attending to their own self-care in meaningful ways, and they would create both a culture and practical means to help them do so.

Systemically, the school and its community would have adequate funding (which requires broader state and federal commitment) to provide for students and their families to have basic needs such as food, clothing, school supplies, and utilities. The school district might even work with the community to ensure that all families have adequate housing needs met. Psychological and counseling needs for all constituents (including school district employees) would be met. All students would feel a sense of belonging and safety because *that* is the culture that has been established by the schools in the district.

It sounds like a lot, we know. It won't happen just because it sounds like something that *should* happen. It would take time and commitment by local, state, and federal agencies, but whatever the goals of the local education system, it all starts with creating a climate for change (Kotter, 1996/2012). We highlight Kotter's first three steps for creating such a climate, which are 1. establishing a sense of urgency, 2. creating the guiding coalition, and 3. developing a vision and strategy.

Three Tenets for Creating a Climate for Trauma-Informed Practices

We have organized this chapter around three basic tenets that correlate with equity in education as defined by Venet (2021) and well-being as defined by the Anthropedia Foundation (2020). Venet defines *equity* in education as:

> Educational equity is the process of ensuring that all students can access high-quality education, that they are fully included in their school communities, that they are able to engage in meaningful and challenging academic work, and that they can do all this in an environment that values them as people. (p. 22)

The Anthropedia Foundation (2020) offers this definition of *well-being*:

> Well-being refers to a state of health, happiness, creativity, vitality, and satisfaction with life. It's more than the presence of positive emotions and the absence of negative ones; it's an inner state of calmness, self-awareness, and self-acceptance that's achieved through a harmonious relationship between one's emotions, thoughts, and actions. (p. 2)

In alignment with these definitions, these tenets center around valuing each person within the education system, from the students to the federal legislators. In Figure 11.1 we situated the tenets within Kotter's (1996/2012) first three steps that are grouped as creating a climate for change. The three tenets for creating a climate for trauma-informed practices are also listed here:

1. The journey to equity begins with a deep dive into each stakeholder's internal beliefs about self-care.
2. Self-care must be a priority; otherwise, caring for students comes at the lasting cost of secondary traumatic stress (STS) and teacher burnout.
3. A sense of well-being must extend beyond the school building and into the community.

Figure 11.1
Three Tenets for Creating a Climate for Trauma-Informed Practices

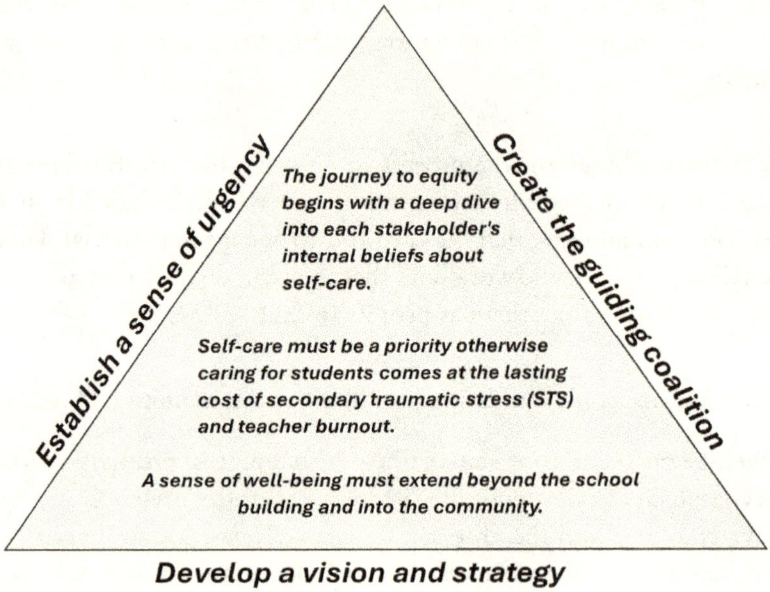

Note: This model incorporates Tenets of Trauma-Informed Practices with Kotter's (2012) first three steps to create a climate for change.

The tenets focus on the well-being of the organization's constituents and stakeholders, acknowledging that equitable well-being must become a cornerstone of a trauma-informed culture. These tenets highlight the need to value each person in the organization.

Who's Helping the Helpers?

As we contemplate anchoring these new approaches, it is important to recognize that we may face obstacles in the path of creating the climate for change that would stall our progress. By following Kotter's (2008) advice to consistently maintain a sense of urgency, we can continue to move forward in the quest for establishing an equitable trauma-informed culture.

Several approaches in change management to support equity and trauma-informed practices have been demonstrated in this book, from the K–12 school chapters written by Haley Porter, Keona Griffin-King, Kasha Roeder, and Joanne Fish, to the post-secondary chapters written by Corinne Mason, Renata Sledge, and Amy Rufus-Doer, to the Community and Systems chapter written by Patricia Carter and Jennifer Brinkmann. Each chapter, in different ways, demonstrated how the demands on the caring professionals in education and community service can lead to secondary traumatic stress, vicarious trauma, and trauma exposure response that Venet (2021) discusses in her book *Equity Centered Trauma-Informed Education* on helping the helpers. Venet discusses the importance of creating a culture of care for the professionals in the school in the same way that a culture of care is created for the students:

> In a community based on an ethic of care, we care for one another, not just the students. The ethic of care is connected to the principle of humanization. Remember, humanization is the foundation for equity-centered trauma-informed practice. An ethic of care attends to the needs of teachers, staff, and students as people. (p. 128)

Attending to Needs

In creating a culture of care, as was discussed in Jamie Doronkin's Chapter 2, the journey to equity can be stalled if we don't believe we have choices or that it is safe to choose ourselves and put our needs for self-care first. One way we want to help the helpers is to offer a set of self-care rights for teachers and students, as one way to begin to establish a norm for self-care and expressing needs.

Self-Care Rights for Teachers

A. My needs are my birthright and mine to learn to know, appreciate, and own through self-care!

B. My needs are my life force! They are how I know I am alive.

C. I have the right to express my needs and have them acknowledged.

D. My feelings about my needs are mine to own and are never a problem.

E. Self-care is a moment-by-moment experience and a basic human right that evolves as I learn and grow.

F. If I feel shame about having needs and caring for myself, I have learned that from others growing up.

G. Modeling my self-care is an important investment for others' growth and learning.

H. Naming and appreciating my needs for self-care create a strong foundation for student safety and their own practice of self-care.

I. My students deserve to know that they can express their self-care needs in a safe environment.

Self-Care Rights for Students

A. My needs are my birthright and mine to learn to know, appreciate, and own through self-care!

B. My needs are my life force! They are how I know I am alive.

C. I have the right to express my needs and have them acknowledged.

D. My feelings about my needs are mine to own and never a problem.

E. Self-care is a moment-by-moment experience and a basic human right that evolves as I learn and grow.

F. If I feel shame about having needs and caring for myself, I have learned that from others.

G. Modeling my self-care is an important way to show others how to help care for me and themselves.

H. Naming and appreciating my needs for self-care create a strong foundation for my own safety and my practice of self-care.

I. Everyone deserves to know that they can express their self-care needs in a safe environment.

A Systemic Approach

The third tenet of this work, "*A sense of well-being must extend beyond school building and the community*," helps us to stay grounded in the argument that this work must be situated within a systemic approach. When improvement plans are initiated by one or a few people in an organization without buy-in from the rest of the stakeholders, they seldom take hold. When improvements are made piecemeal, their impact is generally minimal and short-lived. These "Band-Aid fixes" are usually not sustainable and often cause friction among those involved.

Most teachers have, at one time or another, expressed frustration over having to implement some new mandated initiative that causes additional work and is either too overwhelming to sustain or simply does not work. Hinnant-Crawford (2020) sums up these feelings by naming them "initiative fatigue" (p. 25). These types of mandates are stressful for teachers.

Here we are, promoting yet another initiative—implementing trauma-informed practices in schools. A quick glance at today's news headlines will support the argument for the need for this current call for change, but this is a heavy lift. As our chapter authors have noted, simply attending or providing training on trauma-informed approaches is not enough. We need, as Patricia Carter and Jennifer Brinkmann's Chapter 1 suggests, a systemic approach. Figure 11.2 illustrates the *who* that are impacted in this type of approach and the institutions and systems that create polices that both make this initiative possible and, in some cases, may hinder it.

This figure illustrates how each group of stakeholders, (i.e., students, teachers, support staff, administrators, and parents) and various institutions, (i.e., accrediting bodies, state and federal government agencies, educator preparation programs, and communities) are interconnected through a series of power relations (Smith, 2005, 2006). If we view this systemic structure from the perspective of the *work of learning* (Smith, 2005) that students attempt each day, then we can consider what helps and hinders that work. As we have established that trauma hinders that work, we can then begin to follow the connections illustrated in Figure 11.2 and note where improvements can be made and where additional support is required. Thus, we can begin to apply Kotter's (2012) steps as outlined in *Leading change: With a new preface by the author*, in establishing a systemic culture of trauma-informed practices in our education system.

Figure 11.2
Stakeholders and Institutions that are Interconnected as Part of the Education System

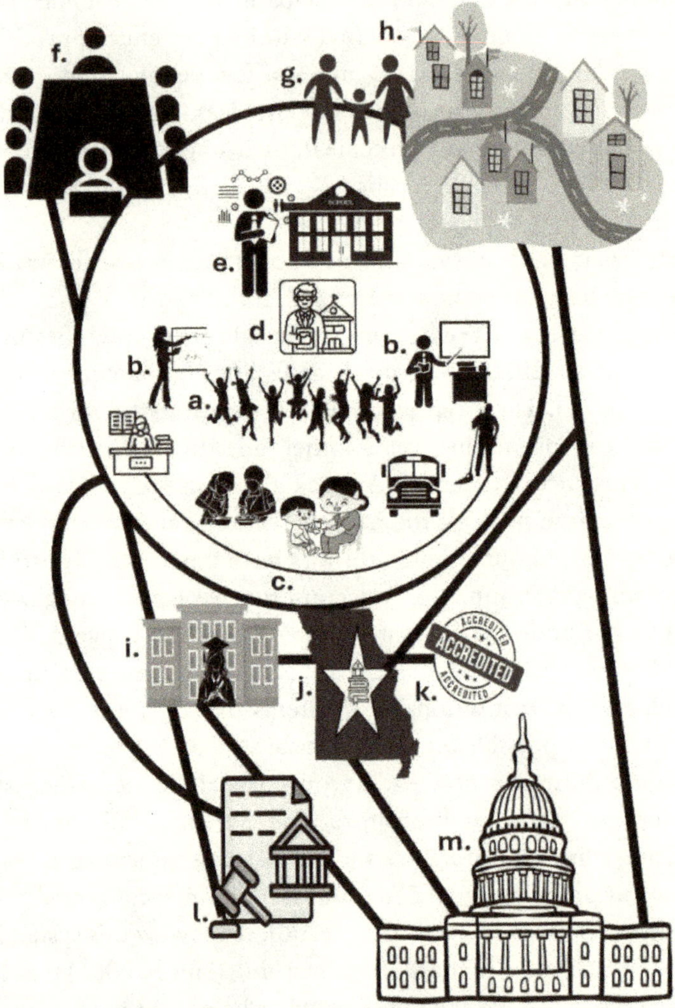

Legend

a. Students
b. Teachers
c. Support Staff
d. Principal (building administrators)
e. Superintendent (district administrators)
f. School Board
g. Family/Parents/Caregivers
h. Community
i. Educator Preparation Programs (EPP)
j. State Department of Education
k. EPP Accreditation Bodies
l. State Legislature
m. Federal Government (Legislature and Department of Education)

Let's think about education as an organization (or an institution). Within this *institution* are a number of stakeholders (represented in Figure 11.2). These stakeholders all play a role in creating the culture of this institution. We must also remember that among these various stakeholders are certain ruling tensions (Smith, 2005, 2006). For example in Figure 11.2 the State Legislature (l) creates statutes that dictate what mandates the State Department of Education (j) places on the state's Educator Preparation Programs (EPPs) (i). At the same time the national Accreditation Body (k), to which the EPP belongs, creates certain standards that the EPP must build into their programs. Also, in some states, the State Department of Education has additional standards that EPPs must adhere to. The teacher candidates who graduate from these programs are trained according to those standards (from the Accreditation Body and the State Department of Education), and they take that training into the schools that hire them.

A 2022 report from the National Association of State Boards of Education (NASBE), stated that as of 2019, 16 states required teachers to receive professional development on trauma (Pierrottet, 2022). However, this training may look different across these states. As was established in Chapter 1, just providing professional development does not necessarily mean that the schools are creating a culture of trauma-informed practices. Perhaps, training needs to take place at the leadership level on how to *create a culture* in trauma-informed training.

Though the idea of nationwide trauma-informed practices is gaining traction, this initiative has not received substantial federal support. As mentioned in Katherina Roeder's Chapter 9, the Trauma-Informed Schools Act has yet to be passed by Congress. This means that even if a State Legislature will fund trauma-informed training for educators, the federal government is not yet establishing a broader culture through legislative or monetary support.

One national entity has stepped up, however. Recently the educator preparation accreditation body, the Association for Advancing Quality in Educator Preparation (AAQEP) revised their standards and added the first standard on trauma: "*Connect students, colleagues, and self to appropriate supports for mental well-being, including those related to trauma*" (AAQEP, 2025, Expectations Framework, Standard 2g). According to Mark LaCelle-Peterson, President and CEO of AAQEP, the topic of trauma is among the top two or three issues AAQEP leadership hear about the most (LaCelle-Peterson, personal communication, August 2, 2024). He said that while previous standards used different language (social-emotional learning), recent events such as the aftermath of the COVID-19 pandemic has brought trauma conversations to the forefront, and the issues around trauma that both students and teachers are experiencing are "just too big to ignore." He said that trauma is "really the challenge" that teachers are facing. He also said that self-care is also an important topic of conversation among educator preparation colleagues.

AAQEP's addition of the trauma-related standard is significant in the quest for systemic change. By including this standard, EPPs who are accredited by AAQEP are required to include trauma-informed competencies in their curriculum and support both hiring schools and graduates who seek additional trauma-informed professional development. Even if the EPP is located in a state that does not require professional development in this area, their programs will include it in order to meet this standard. This is an example of moving towards systemic change. It follows Kotter's (1996/2012) first set of steps that are meant to create a climate for change by creating a sense of urgency; the standard must be met, or at least the EPP must be making plans to meet the standard. In this case, AAQEP is one of the guiding coalitions, which in turn pushes the EPP to become a steward for the cause, and develop a vision, strategy, and means for meeting this new standard.

Self-Care and Resilience Resources

This section includes resources for self-care and building resilience that range from curriculum and programs to books, webinars, classes, and activities. While we are not recommending or promoting a specific product, these well-known and empirically established resources are offered as potential tools to support an organization's journey toward equity in trauma-informed practices.

Mindfulness-Based Stress Reduction (MBSR)

One of the most applied definitions of mindfulness is provided by Jon Kabat-Zinn (1994), who suggests that mindfulness can be described as a moment-to-moment awareness cultivated by purposefully paying attention to the present experience without judgment. Mindfulness-Based Stress Reduction (MBSR) was developed by Dr. Kabat-Zinn in 1979 and is a well-established mindfulness training program that helps to reduce stress, depression, and anxiety (Kabat-Zinn, 2003). This curriculum has been empirically replicated in international populations, including with those in the health care profession, as well as continuing education students and college undergraduates. "Mindfulness-Based Stress Reduction teaches individuals to observe situations and thoughts in a nonjudgmental, nonreactive, and accepting manner and provides training in formal mindfulness practices, including body scan, sitting meditation, and yoga" (Khoury et al., 2015, p. 519).

Mindfulness-Based Stress Reduction is now taught in every state in the US and more than 30 countries. The standard MBSR course includes eight weekly sessions of two to three hours each and an all-day session after the sixth week that involves a full day of mindfulness practice in a modified retreat format. Websites such as MBSR Training by Jon Kabat-Zinn - Mindfulness Training at https://mbsrtraining.org provide more information on this program and training.

Teaching Mindfulness Skills to Kids and Teens

Another mindfulness resource is the book *Teaching Mindfulness Skills to Kids and Teens*, edited by Dr. Christopher Willard and Dr. Amy Saltzman (2015). Some chapters in this book are specifically dedicated to working with elementary-school-age children, teens, children who have special needs, and diverse populations. Other chapters are focused on yoga, movement and dance, and mindfulness in sports, art, and games. Additional chapters focus on the science of mindfulness, executive functioning, and neurobiological models of meditation and practices.

The Online Compassion Course and Book

The Compassion Book: Lessons from the Compassion Course (Bond, 2017) is filled with specific ideas and practical steps that provide the "how to" of compassion (p. ix). Based on the lessons from the 52-week (non-graded) asynchronous online Compassion Course: The Compassion Course Online at https://www.compassioncourse.org that Thom Bond created, each chapter features (1) a concept, (2) a story to illustrate the concept, and (3) practices to help put the concept into action. The book and course also contain a series of resources that includes:

- Feelings: list of feelings associated with met needs, such as affection, excitement, gratitude, happiness, and inspiration
- Feelings: list of feelings associated with unmet needs, such as anger, confusion, disconnection, fear, and sadness
- Needs and Values: list of things we all want in our lives, such as autonomy, connection, meaning, and peace
- Exercises and steps to help shift toward compassion and translate judgments into observations

The Resilient Practitioner

In the fourth edition of their book, *The Resilient Practitioner*, Thomas Skovholt and Michelle Trotter-Mathison (2025) provide chapters filled with theory, empirical evidence on self-care, practitioner insights on professional thriving and resilience, case studies, vignettes, strategies, tips, and exercises for self-reflection. The book is designed for all practitioners, including teachers, instructors, advisors, therapists, social workers, counselors, psychologists, and other service professionals such as law enforcement professionals, attorneys, dentists, physicians, and occupational and physical therapists. It has chapters specifically devoted to self-care and caring for others, resilience, and speaks to the concepts of "boundaried generosity" (p. 3) and "the good enough practitioner" (p. 160) as keys for helping practitioners on their way to professional resilience. The book includes multiple resources, such as a resilience inventory and a self-care action plan.

Equity-Centered Trauma-Informed Education

In her book *Equity-Centered Trauma-Informed Education*, Alex Shervin Venet (2021) provides practical, affirming, and proactive strategies for supporting trauma-informed practices with a focus on social justice and educational equity. As a teacher herself, Venet provides principles and perspective shifts toward transforming schools to respond to trauma with what she calls "rubber-meets-the-road strategies" (p. xix). She shares that the primary role of a trauma-informed teacher should be that of "connection builder" (p. 115), discusses the importance of caring for the self while caring for others, and cautions school leaders to be aware of what she calls "cutesy wellness" (p. 135). Venet also offers an equity-centered policy review tool (pp. 148–149) that generates questions to promote reflective consideration of current policies using an equity and trauma-informed lens.

References

Anthropedia Foundation. (2020). *Anthropedia module: Know yourself part one*, 2. https://anthropedia.org

Association for Advancing Quality in Educator Preparation (AAQEP). (2025). Expectations framework, Standard 2g.

Bond. T. (2017). *The Compassion Book: Lessons from the Compassion Course*. One Human Publishing.

Hinnant-Crawford, B. (2020). *Improvement Science in Education*. Myers Education Press.

Kabat-Zinn J. (1994). *Wherever you go, there you are: Mindfulness meditation in everyday life*. Hyperion.

Kabat-Zinn, J. (2003). Mindfulness-based stress reduction (MBSR). *Constructivism in the human sciences*, *8*(2), 73.

Khoury, B., Sharma, M., Rush, S. E., & Fournier, C. (2015). Mindfulness-based stress reduction for healthy individuals: A meta-analysis. *Journal of psychosomatic research*, *78*(6), 519-528.

Kotter, J. P. (1996). *Leading change*. Harvard Business School Press.

Kotter, J. P. (2008). *A sense of urgency*. Harvard Business Press.

Kotter, J. P. (2012). *Leading change*: *With a new preface by the author*. Harvard Business School Press.

Missouri Department of Elementary and Secondary Education (2019). *The Missouri model for trauma-informed schools*. http://missouri-model-trauma-informed-schools.pdf

Pierrottet, C. (2022). Building trauma-informed school systems. *National Association of State Board of Education, 29*(3), 1-2 .

Skovholt, T. M., & Trotter-Mathison, M. (2025) *The resilient practitioner: Burnout and compassion fatigue prevention and self-care strategies for the helping professions* (4th ed). Routledge.

Smith, D. E. (2005). *Institutional ethnography: A sociology for people*. AltaMira Press.

Smith, D. E. (2006). *Institutional ethnography as practice*. Rowman & Littlefield Publishers, Inc.

Venet, A. S. (2021). *Equity-centered trauma-informed education*. W.W. Norton and Co.

Willard, C., & Saltzman, A. (Eds). (2015). *Teaching mindfulness skills to kids and teens*. Guilford Press.

ABOUT THE AUTHORS

Joanne Fish, PhD is an Associate Dean of Humanities at Jefferson College in Hillsboro, Missouri. She has worked in education for the past two decades. Before assuming her current role as Associate Dean, Dr. Fish worked in teacher preparation for ten years and, in multiple settings, has researched trauma's impact on learning. She is also a reading specialist who has worked with elementary, middle school, secondary, and college students who have found reading challenging. She holds a PhD in literacy education from the University of Missouri–Columbia, a master's degree in education from William Woods University in Fulton, MO, and a master's degree in communication and a bachelor's degree in English from Pittsburg State University in Pittsburg, KS. She enjoys spending time with her grown children: Tabitha, Kiefer, and Savanna, as well as each of her three grandchildren: Sylei, Landon, and Lyncoln. Dr. Fish lives in St. Louis, MO with her three dogs, four cats, and 90-lb. sulcata tortoise named Mr. T.

Jamie Doronkin, PhD is currently a Professor Emeritus and Adjunct Instructor at Fontbonne University in St. Louis, MO. She most recently served as the Director for the Fontbonne EdD Program in Collaborative High Impact Instruction and was the co-developer of the EdD program at Fontbonne. Dr. Doronkin has earned dual bachelors' degrees in Special Education and Elementary Education from Oklahoma Christian University, a master's degree in special education from the University of Central Oklahoma, and a doctoral degree in Special Education with a secondary transition focus from the University of Oklahoma. Research interests for Dr. Doronkin include trauma-informed and trauma-sensitive educator preparation practices, adverse childhood experiences (ACEs), adverse community experiences, and the impact of these adverse experiences on learning and brain development. Dr. Doronkin has presented locally, regionally, and nationally on self-care survival strategies; IEP meeting behaviors; and family and sibling disability-related dynamics that include the impact of trauma, transition into adulthood, and self-determination and self-advocacy for individuals with disabilities. Her most recent studies and training include body-centered and somatic movement therapy practices.

Jennifer Brinkmann, MBA was the founding president of Alive and Well Communities (AWC), formed in 2017 to address the impact of trauma and toxic stress across the State of Missouri. AWC grew to include infrastructure in St. Louis, Kansas City, and Southeast Missouri. The work of AWC in St. Louis began at the St. Louis Regional Health Commission (RHC), where Jennifer was Chief of Staff. In 2023, Alive and Well Communities merged back with the RHC. At that time, the organization supported schools, communities, social service providers, and healthcare organizations in becoming trauma-informed. AWC had more than 500 volunteers across Missouri and reached more than 40,000 residents with programming. Prior to joining the RHC in 2010, Jennifer worked for 15 years in branding, marketing, and communication, supporting a range of clients, including those working to make St. Louis a stronger, healthier region for all. Today, she is the i-Team director leading innovation for the City of St. Louis as part of the Bloomberg American Sustainable Cities initiative. Jennifer earned her undergraduate degree from Stephens College and an MBA from Washington University in St. Louis.

Patricia Carter, PhD is an adjunct professor at University of Missouri–Columbia, College of Education's Educational, School and Counseling Psychology Program teaching graduate courses related to trauma, mental health, and child maltreatment, as well as supervising graduate capstone projects. She received her doctorate in clinical psychology from the University of Mississippi. Dr. Carter spent most of her career at the Missouri Dept. of Mental Health (DMH) in both clinical and administrative positions focusing on child mental health and addressing system issues impacting access and quality. While there she led the work on trauma and developed the Missouri Trauma Roundtable which created the MO Model: A Developmental Framework for Trauma Informed and related documents. After retiring from DMH, Dr. Carter was an assistant professor at the University of Missouri–Columbia Dept. of Psychiatry and started the Center for Excellence in Child Well-Being which provides clinical and systems consultation. Simultaneously, she began her current role with the College of Education. Throughout her career, Dr. Carter has been a vocal advocate for children with mental health needs and their families.

Keona Griffin-King, EdD has 30 years of experience working with youth. Her career began in 1996 as an after-school specialist and mentor with the YWCA in St. Louis, MO. She is currently a life coach and high school teacher. She has dedicated her life's work to reframing the perception of youth with challenging behaviors to "youth overcoming life's challenges." With a BA in Psychology, an MBA, an MAT, and a Doctorate in Education, Dr. Griffin-King specializes in trauma-informed practices, emotional regulation, and behavior modification. Her work includes developing tools, courses, and training programs that empower students and teachers to navigate challenges and thrive. Her educational thrusts are culturally responsive teaching and blending emotional regulation strategies with academic skills to foster resilience, agency, advocacy, and equity for all students in all learning spaces.

Corinne Wohlford Mason, PhD is an associate professor of American Studies and chair of Women's and Gender Studies at Saint Louis University. Before joining the Saint Louis University faculty in 2023, she taught for 24 years in English, creative writing, history, and interdisciplinary studies at Fontbonne University, where she also held a variety of administrative posts. Dr. Mason has held other appointments at Washington University, Maryville University, and the University of Missouri—St. Louis and taught high school in Japan. Dr. Mason holds an MFA in writing from Washington University and a PhD in American studies from Saint Louis University. Her scholarship focuses on the intersections of neoliberalism, race, and sentiment in US culture, and her poetry has been featured in *Bennington Review*, *Harvard Review*, *Phoebe*, *New Ohio Review*, and several other journals. In 2022, her poem "On Taiko" was nominated for a Pushcart Prize. Although she is not a Saint Louis native, Dr. Mason is a loyal advocate for and historian of the city. She regularly partners with St. Louis institutions—including the Missouri History Museum, where she serves as a contract public historian; the Ulysses S. Grant National Historic Site; the Jefferson National Parks Association; and many others—to advance honest and reflective historical interpretation of Saint Louis.

Haley Porter, EdD teaches in the St. Louis Public School district and is a former police officer. Her experiences working on cases primarily involving children and victims of domestic abuse inform her approach to addressing the trauma that students face each year. She has developed a school-wide care closet to meet students' needs and serves as the content team leader in her middle school. Through these roles, she promotes a sense of belonging and community among her students. Dr. Porter earned her Master of Teaching from Missouri Baptist University and her Doctor of Education degree in Collaborative High Impact Instruction from Fontbonne University. Her primary research interest is to better prepare students, particularly those in low socioeconomic areas, for life after the classroom.

Katherina M. Roeder, EdD is an accomplished educator specializing in special education and Universal Design for Learning (UDL). She serves as a Modified Reading Teacher for Special School District of St. Louis County, utilizing evidence-based strategies and trauma-informed practices to support her students. Driven by a passion for empowering every student to reach their full potential, she believes that education is the key to breaking barriers and building brighter futures. Dr. Roeder earned her Doctor of Education degree in Collaborative High Impact Instruction and has authored work on equity and trauma-informed education. Residing in St. Louis, Missouri, she is committed to advancing inclusive education and lifelong learning.

Amy Ruffus-Doerr, PhD is an Associate Professor & Co-Chair of Biological & Behavioral Sciences at Fontbonne University. She earned her PhD in Educational Psychology from the University of Missouri–St. Louis. Dr. Ruffus-Doerr has worked on ten different research projects, including research on teacher epistemology, the educational experience of African American males, and educating for the Knowledge Age. She is the founder of Peer Support Allies, a program developed to address the mental health crisis by leveraging peers to increase help-seeking behaviors in traditionally marginalized groups.

Renata Sledge, PhD, LCSW is a licensed clinical social worker and assistant professor in the School of Social Work at the University of Missouri–St. Louis. Dr. Sledge brings her understanding of inter-relatedness to inform research and clinical practice to better understand how belonging can impact quality of life, promote positive family adjustment, and disease management for people impacted by chronic conditions. Through research defined by interdisciplinary collaboration, Dr. Sledge has published and presented on areas including medical decision-making, ethics, and the role of relationships in well-being. Dr. Sledge graduated with a PhD in Medical Family Therapy from the Saint Louis University School of Medicine.

INDEX